T0339766

OLD SHANGHAI AND THE CLASH OF REVOLUTION

OLD SHANGHAI AND THE CLASH OF REVOLUTION

X. L. WOO

Algora Publishing
New York

Library of Congress Cataloging-in-Publication Data —

Woo, X. L.
   Old Shanghai and the clash of revolution / X.L. Woo.
     pages cm
   Includes bibliographical references and index.
     ISBN 978-0-87586-996-4 (soft cover: alk.paper) — ISBN 978-0-87586-
997-1 (hard cover: alk. paper) — ISBN 978-0-87586-998-8 (ebook) 1. Woo, X.
L. 2. Woo, X. L.—Family. 3. Shanghai (China)—Biography. 4. Revolutions—
Social aspects—China—Shanghai—History—20th century. 5. Shanghai
(China)—Social life and customs—20th century. 6. English teachers—
China—Shanghai—Biography. 7. China—History—1949-1976—Biography. 8.
China—History—1976-2002—Biography. 9. Authors, Chinese—Biography. 10.
Immigrants—United States—Biography. I. Title.
   DS796.S253W66 2013
   951'.13205092—dc23
   [B]
                              2013009620

Printed in the United States

Table of Contents

CHAPTER 1 – A SHANGHAI FAMILY ON THE EVE OF WAR

"Wa– –!" the cry of a baby boy was heard in Zhongde Hospital in Shanghai. It was 3:35 in the morning, on the 15th day of the 1st moon of the lunar calendar, in the year of ox, 1937. The cry of a newborn baby is the omen given to every individual, warning that life is bitter. If life were always happy, the first sound a baby issues would be laughter, not crying.

Half a year after the baby was born, smoldering skirmishes burst into flame with the Anti-Japanese War (which the West calls the Second Sino-Japanese War). Total war broke out with the so-called Lugou Bridge Event outside Peking, on the seventh of July (07/07), 1937. Chinese people remember it as the Double-Seventh Event. Life in Shanghai went on as usual; however, these scenes played out against a backdrop of shifting political maneuvers that eventually melded into the Pacific side of World War II, shattering the structures and burning off the patina that for centuries had made "Old Shanghai" a world unto itself.

At the outbreak of the war, Germany, Russia and the United States aided China against Imperial Japan, even as China was deeply divided between Chiang Kai-shek's Kuomintang and Mao's Communist Party. As the years went by, alliances shifted and more and more of the country felt the terrible impact of war. But for now, in Shanghai, those maneuverings took place high overhead and the rich simply went on enjoying their merry making, while the poor went on struggling to keep alive, as always.

Wu Renbao, the father of the baby, was born in 1895 and while he was still in Ningpo, a city just south of Shanghai, he had married a girl named Yunxian from the Wang family, under an arrangement made by his parents, shortly after the fall of the last imperial dynasty in China. Now the country was experimenting with Western social and economic ideas; but marriage was still arranged by parents; there was no freedom to select one's own spouse like nowadays. The girl was short and plain, and besides that, was a year older than Mr. Wu. He did not like her. They often bickered. Neighbors attributed their quarrels to the fact that the wife was born in the year of the rooster and the husband in the year of dog. The pronunciation of the Chinese characters for rooster and dog sound like the noise of quarreling; therefore, people believe that such a couple will often bicker.

Anyway, in 1913, at the age of 18, Mr. Wu had gone to Shanghai to become an apprentice to a dye merchant, who bought barrels of dye from abroad and repacked it in small boxes to sell to stores and factories to dye cloth. After three years, when he finished his apprenticeship, he started his own business in 1916 as a dye merchant with some friends, in a sort of partnership.

Every month he sent money to Ningpo for the support of his wife and his first son, Wu Dehua, born in 1926. When he opened his own business, he rented a house. In Shanghai all the houses were built along a lane, divided into side lanes. Along either side of the side lanes were row houses, each sharing its side walls with the next house, just like townhouse in the U.S., and without trees or lawns in the lane or side lanes. The lanes were paved with cement.

There were two types of houses: one with bathrooms and the other without. People used wooden stools, like small barrels with covers, for their natural duties. Every morning, a worker would push a covered wooden cart through the lanes, crying "Bring out your stools." And the housewives or servants would do so. After pouring the contents of the stools into the covered cart, they washed the stools by the gutter alongside the front of the houses. The stools would be set against the wall to dry before being taken back into the houses.

There was another way to differentiate the houses. There were generally three types: single-room houses, generally three-storeyed, with only one bedroom on every floor; double-room houses with two bedrooms on every floor; and triple-room houses, with three bedrooms on every floor. The two-room and three-room houses generally had two storeys.

Mr. Wu rented a house without bathroom, two storeyed. Mr. Wu used the ground floor as the shop and the second floor as his living quarters. He sent for his wife and son to come to Shanghai, and they all lived upstairs since there were two bedrooms. As his business developed, he took on some apprentices and rented another house across the side lane, using the ground floor as a warehouse and the second floor as lodging for the apprentices. He also hired a male cook to prepare three meals for his family and the apprentices. Every day when his partners came, they had lunch at Mr. Wu's expense.

When Dehua was seven years old, he acquired a brother named Wu Dinghua, who was born in 1933.

Mr. Wu was destined to have a second wife as he did not like his first wife, who had been dumped on him by his parents. At that time, a man could have as many wives as he wanted — or as many as he could support. When the wives lived together, the first wife was called wife and the others were called concubines. But when a second wife lived separately, she was called wife, too. Second wives always came from poor families, or they would not marry men who were much older and accept the secondary role. But the second wife was always the one the husband liked better, or he would not have married her. If a man had several wives, they would vie for his favor. The most favored wife, generally a concubine, would receive more gifts of money or jewels and would accompany the man everywhere he went when a wife was needed for the occasion.

By chance Mr. Wu met a beautiful girl 20 years of age, who was demure and quiet. He fell in love with her at first sight. The girl, whose family name was also Wang, was born in 1913. The girl's family was poor. Her father had died early of some disease. Her mother took in laundry and did other jobs for wealthy people. She had a sister one year younger.

Then Mr. Wu rented a room in a big house in another neighborhood and lived there with the girl, whose name was Zhengming. The girl was 18 years younger than he. In Chinese tradition, it was deemed not good for the husband and wife to have an age difference of six years. Superstitions said this would mean they had conflicting fates. Thus, with a difference of 18 years in age, three times six years, one might expect there to be great conflicts in their fates. But, no, according to a fortune-teller, since the difference, or the "age distance," as the fortune-teller put it, was so great, even a cannon ball could not reach the other side. So it was safe. Since then, Wu no longer lived with his first wife. Every morning he came to work in his shop and every evening he went to his second wife, and he stayed with his new wife on weekends, meaning Sundays. At that time in China people had to work on Saturdays.

Four years afterwards, he had his third son, by this wife. And that was the baby boy whose cry opened our story, which is, in fact, his story. He was named Wu Genghua. Mr. Wu liked this son better than the other two, since he was born to the beloved wife. There is a Chinese saying that goes, "Love the house, love the crow nesting on the house." Maybe it is equivalent to the English saying, "Love me, love my dog." Mr. Wu went to a fortune-teller to have the baby's fate foretold, and he said that the baby would grow up to be a man of talent, but without much money all his life. And he would be often sick till the age of sixteen.

Genghua was four years younger than the second son. As the mother was still too young to take good care of the baby, it was given to the care of Mrs. Wang, her mother, who hired a wet nurse to feed the baby. The father gave money to Mrs. Wang (we'll call her Granny, hereafter), and now she did not need to work anymore. The baby's right foot was a little crooked. Granny massaged his foot most of the day for many months till the foot became normal in shape. When Genghua was one year of age, the wet nurse was sent away. Now he was a toddler. Granny could feed him soup or porridge or juice. At that time rich people could buy milk powder in tins with the brand KLIM. So Granny also fed the child with the milk powder in hot water for better nourishment.

Granny's second daughter was also pretty and she married a man at the age of eighteen. He was a businessman, also much older than she. The best way for pretty girls from poor families was always to marry a man of wealth, but much older. Now Granny lived alone with the child, and she loved him very much. She was a warm-hearted woman, but she was also very strict.

Granny had bought a girl of ten as a maidservant. She was given three meals a day, nothing more. When Genghua had an orange or candy, the girl stood aside to watch him eating, swallowing her saliva. Once when Granny was not at home, Genghua saw the girl eat some sugar, using her finger to dip into the sugar jar and leaving her fingerprint on the surface of the sugar. When Granny came back and wanted to use sugar for cooking, she found the fingerprint. Granny flared up. She could not bear anyone stealing anything. If the girl had asked her for sugar, she might perhaps have given her a spoonful. But no stealing. So she ordered the girl to kneel on the floor by the table and beat her bare bottom with a ruler. Then she sold the girl to someone else, afraid that when the girl grew up, she might steal something valuable.

When Genghua was growing teeth, according to tradition his grandma would put a steamed bun on the cover of the stool without Genghua seeing it. It was said that the steamed bun was offered to the tooth god. But why it should be placed on the cover of the stool, Genghua never asked and never knew. However, a small child seeing such a treat would naturally take it and eat it. The offering to the tooth god might be helpful to the growth of the teeth when eaten.

In 1940, Mr. Wu rented a whole second floor — two bedrooms and an independent toilet — in another house on Avenue Joffre, in the upscale French Concession. Originally this road was named

West River Road, and in 1906, its name was changed to Route Paul Brunat. In June of 1915, it was changed again to Avenue Joffre, after the French general who came to Shanghai in March of 1922 to lead the ceremony for raising a monument. In 1943 when the Wang Jingwei government took over Shanghai, the name was changed again to Taishan Road. Wang Jingwei was the chairman of Japan's puppet government in China. After the surrender of Japan in October of 1945, it was renamed as Linsen Road. Lin Sen had been the chairman of the central government before the Japanese invasion of China. Then communist government came to Shanghai, and on May 25, 1950, it was finally called Central Huaihai Road. Huaihai is the name of a river in the eastern part of China where a critical battle took place between November 1948 and January 1949, with the Communist Party under the leadership of Mao against the National Party under Chiang Kai-shek. The Communist Party was victorious. They named this road in memory of their victory.

As now Mr. Wu had two bedrooms, he let Granny move in so she could live with her elder daughter and the daughter could always be close to her son. They hired a girl, Ahmei by name, to do all the housework. The girl was more than ten years older than Genghua. The house had a decorative balcony on the second floor outside the bathroom, but without any door. The only access was through the bathroom window. Once, when Genghua was five years old, Granny bought some young chicks and during the daytime, the girl let the chicks down onto the balcony through the window, but in the evening, the chicks had to be shut up in a big box for the night. However, the chicks could not come in by themselves. Therefore, Genghua had his first adventure, as he had to go out the window and catch the chicks one by one and hand them to the girl at the window, who put chicks into the box. Then the boy was lifted up into the toilet through the window.

As Genghua was often ill, a friend of Mr. Wu's suggested that the boy should be given up, in name only, of course, to be the son of God Guan, who had been a general of Shu Kingdom in the Three Kingdoms period. As a general, Guan had been a good and brave man, always loyal to the emperor. People had worshiped him posthumously as a god. Many gods in China were thus created, a tradition lasting till the so-called Cultural Revolution when Mao was worshiped like a living god. In almost all the Chinese restaurants, especially in Hong Kong, statuettes of God Guan were put somewhere to be worshiped. But no such tradition was kept in restaurants in the mainland. There was a temple with his statue in it, called God Guan Temple, not far from Genghua's house. It was said that the thirteenth day of the fifth moon was his birthday. On that day many people went to worship him. Granny took the boy to the temple and after the worshiping and certain procedures the boy got an amulet to carry on his person, which would protect him from evil things, including illness. Now he was a son of God Guan and was given a new name, Guanming — which only his grandma used.

There were many pedlars selling all kinds of things on the sidewalk before the temple, such as small wooden swords, spears, knives on long sticks, and triangular banners on thin wooden sticks for boys, and little colored beads, mirrors and combs for girls. Genghua bought a knife on a long stick, which was supposed to represent the weapon the god Guan used in fighting on battlefields. At home Genghua sat astride a bench as his horse and brandished the knife, as if he were the god Guan in fighting.

Once Granny took Genghua to the temple of the city god. There was a pedlar selling goldfish. Their tails looked like gauze skirts spreading in the water, so lovely and beautiful. Genghua importuned Granny to buy a couple for him. But before long, the goldfish died because Genghua fed them too much.

One day, since the wife did not work, she took Genghua to a public park where they rode on a horse-drawn open carriage. There was also a miniature train for children. Sometimes in the evening the parents would take the boy to watch horse races or dog races.

Mr. Wu had a friend called Gan Dounan, who wanted investors for his Lixing Hot Water Bottle Factory. His main brand, the Great Wall, was famous in Shanghai. Mr. Wu obliged by making an investment there and was elected one of the seven members of Board of Trustees. Mr. Wu always liked to help friends with their enterprises and also invested in Xinyi Pharmaceutical Factory, Changming Clock Factory, and some other factories. However, he was opposed to the Stock Market. Once in a board meeting of the Lixing Hot Water Bottle company, someone proposed selling company stock in the market, but Mr. Wu was opposed, saying that many people committed suicide after losing money in the stock market. The stock market was seen as an evil thing, as it sucked in many innocent lives to feed a few greedy ones.

When Mr. Wu was in his shop, his new wife would play with the boy. She would hold her hands before a lamp and cast shadows on the opposite wall. When her fingers and thumbs in different positions in the air, different shadows would appear on the wall, some looking like a rabbit, some like a bird or a dog, etc. Sometimes she told him stories. Once she told him a story of her own experience. It was about a fox genie she had witnessed. One day when she was ten years old, when her mother had gone out to buy vegetables, she stayed in their room upstairs. Then she heard some unusual noise in the room. Being jumpy and easily frightened, like many girls, she ran downstairs, and something hanging on the wall fell and followed her, rolling down the staircase. She rushed through the kitchen and out the back door. She stayed outside waiting for her mother. She would go in with her mother when she was back. But meantime, she peeped inside to see what the matter was in the house. To her surprise and fear, she saw a woman's figure standing against the wall facing the staircase. All of a sudden she thought of a story she had once heard, about a fox genie. She did not even dare to keep looking at the figure. After a while, when she peeped again, nothing was there. The woman must have been gone. Since it was a strange woman she had never seen before, she believed that it was a fox genie. Could it been a ghost? No. Because ghosts cannot appear in the daylight, according to traditional belief.

Genghua had a variety of toys including a mechanical, moving chick made of tin plate. When the key was wound, the chick would peck rice on the table. He had a dog of the same kind, which could be wound up and then it would turn round and round, wagging its tail. Then he had a little pipe or horn of rolled up paper with a brightly colored feather at its tip. When he blew air into it, it would stretch out straight and long. Genghua liked to blow it and tickle his grandma on the cheek. This was Genghua's favorite toy.

Chapter 2 – Life Under Japanese Occupation

In 1944, Shanghai was still under the occupation of Japan, but life went on and business went on, with some difference of course. For the well-to-do, Shanghai had long been a cosmopolitan city with many Western influences. Mr. Wu had saved some money and bought a house in a lane on Taishan Road, former Avenue Joffre. The house had three storeys and was a single-room type. For the purchase of a house at that time in Shanghai, the buyer should pay the price with gold bars. Generally there were two sorts of gold bars: big ones and small ones. The big gold bar weighed ten taels and the small gold bar one tael. In Shanghai slang, the big gold bar was called the big yellow fish and the small gold bar the small yellow fish. Mr. Wu paid ten big gold bars for it. The design of the house was like this: one big room on every floor, and two small mezzanine rooms, one between the ground floor and the second floor, in which Granny lived, and the other between the second floor and the third floor, which was used as a storage room. The big room on the ground floor served as the living room as well as dining room. There was a big square table at one end of the room and a set of leather sofas at the other end. An icebox stood in one corner beside the table. Big pieces of ice were ordered to put in the box with a metal container under the box to hold the water of the melted ice. On the mantelpiece porcelain vases and other ornaments were displayed.

In one corner of the other end against the wall, there was a small long table, on which stood a tiny shrine with a statuette of Buddha inside. An incense burner and two candlesticks were laid before it. On the first and the fifteenth day of every moon, Mr. Wu would burn some incense and a pair of candles, and chanted some Buddhist sutras as a routine, before he went to the shop. Sometimes, Mr. Wu had a quick temper. If anyone did something wrong when he was chanting sutras, he would stop chanting and scold the wrongdoer, then go back to chanting again. The servants would joke about it among themselves that if chanting of the sutras would go to Buddha, Buddha would receive it together with the scolding words.

Mr. And Mrs. Wu slept in the big room on the second floor with a bathroom attached, which had two doors, one opened to the bedroom and the other to the landing. The bedroom had a set of rosewood furniture, a big bed in the middle with one end against the wall. Beside the big bed, a cot was set up for the boy to sleep in at night. There was a glass door in a corner that opened to the small balcony, overlooking the side lane. The balcony of the next house was connected with only a low wall partition. The family next door had a boy one year older than Genghua. Genghua and the boy next door used the balconies to exchange books both liked to read. They handed books over round the wall partition to each other. They were playmates.

The big room on the third floor was used as a servants' dormitory in because a middle-aged woman and a man in his thirties had come to Shanghai from Ningpo, Mr. Wu's homeland. The girl Ahmei still worked for the family, who was now a young woman. She and the woman slept on the third floor. The man used a camp bed for the night in the living room. The woman and the man both coming from Ningpo looked like lovers, but they did not do anything wrong or show any intimacy to each other in front of others. At that time in China, any intimate behavior in public between servants was against tradition and would cause them trouble.

Since the new house was big, Mr. Wu had his second son, Dinghua, move in to sleep in the servant's room. But a curtain was hung up in the middle to separate the room into two parts. The women slept behind the curtain and the second son in the front section close to the door. He and Genghua both went to primary school for education. The primary school Genghua went to was an affiliated one of the famous Qixiu Female Middle School, which was just located across Avenue Joffre from the lane Wu family lived in. The middle school was changed to be the Shanghai Twelfth Female Middle School after the Communist Party came. The primary school was no longer affiliated and moved to First Ruijing Road and was called the Shanghai First Primary School of First Ruijing Road.

Meanwhile a tutor came to give the boys private lessons on classics and calligraphy. Mr. Wu, when a child, was sent to a local private school to study classics and calligraphy. Therefore, he thought that such education was very important to his sons as the modern education system never gave enough lessons on classics and calligraphy. Since Mr. Wu was always away from home attending to his business, the second son often played truant. The tutor didn't want to tell Mr. Wu, afraid that he would beat the boy and the boy would hate him. The new wife could not be too strict with the second son as he was not her son. If she maltreated him, which she would certainly not do, the first wife would get angry. Only Genghua loved classics and calligraphy. It seemed that the tutor was teaching Genghua alone. Genghua began to practice the writing of classical poems and essays for the tutor to correct. The tutor thought Genghua a language genius and often praised him for his swift improvement.

The relationship between the wives was okay. Whenever they met, they would be polite to each other and talked a little. The husband would never tolerate quarrels between them. So the new wife treated the second son nicely. The first son still lived with his mother. He would sometimes come to see his father. As Mr. Wu was always strict on his sons and gave them very little pocket money, the new wife often gave some more money to the first son since he was a teenager and had more allowance. So the first son liked her and respected her. Generally in old China, the children of the first wife did not often respect the second wife or concubines, especially when a bad relationship existed between the first wife and concubines. The first son called the new wife Auntie because she was not much older than he. But the second son called her mother since he lived together with her and was much younger than the first son. Based on the age she could be his mother. In old China, sometimes the sons or daughters of the first wife were even older than the concubines. So they were not willing to call such a young concubine mother. But in feudal China, the sons or daughters of the first wife had to kowtow to the concubines even if they were younger than they, and call them Second Mother, or Third Mother, etc. If they refused to do so or showed reluctance, they would be beaten by the father. It was the tradition.

The older woman from Ningpo did the cooking and Ahmei did the cleaning. The man did the shopping. The Japanese invaders issued ID papers to every resident in Shanghai. A fingerprint was printed on the left upper corner of the ID paper. Then printed on it were many coupons. The Japanese allotted rice rations to residents in Shanghai. When people went to get rice, a coupon on the ID paper was cut off. Rice was given out only based on the count of coupons. The manservant of the Wu family was sent to bring back the rice ration. He would spend a lot of time waiting in line before he could get it. The rice was mostly not whole, only broken bits, but it was okay to cook and eat. The residents were assigned another duty. Every family had to have a person standing in the street near the house as a guardsman. He was given a whistle and if anything unusual happened, he had to blow the whistle and Japanese soldiers would appear immediately, out of nowhere. So the manservant performed this duty as well.

There lived a Japanese family just across the side lane to the house of Mr. Wu. They ignored all other neighbors, and the neighbors kept at a respectful distance from the family. Once the Japanese man, supposedly the head of the family, rode home on a jinricksha. When he got down from it, he went directly to his house without paying the puller, who asked for the money due to him, of course. However, the Japanese man boxed his ears till his nose bled.

Simultaneously he abused the puller in his mother tongue that none of the bystanders understood. The rickshaw puller had to run off for fear of his dear life.

The Japanese feared that the US airplanes would come to bombard Shanghai. They gave orders that every house should not show light at night. For that purpose every lamp in the house had to be wrapped all around with black cloth. The lamp could only illuminate downward. If any light showed from the house, they would come to warn the family.

Mr. Wu was more and more fond of playing mahjong, and that is a game that requires four players. If the friends gathered at Mr. Wu's house, a heavy black curtain would be drawn tightly to prevent light from leaking out. The lamp only shed enough light for the mahjong table. Once two policemen came to knock at the door. The mahjong players were frightened. But the policemen did not come in. They just asked some routine questions and left. In fact, the Japanese did not care about people playing mahjong. What they cared was people resisting them.

That year, Mr. Wu's young wife got pregnant again. This was the fourth child for the Wu family. The following year, on August 15, 1945, Japan surrendered and the Second World War ended. But until the Chinese army took over Shanghai, the Japanese soldiers kept law and order in the city. One day, a Japanese officer was walking in the street and some boys threw stones at his back. The officer turned round angrily and drew his sword half out of the sheath. The boys ran away and the officer went his way. If it had happened before the surrender of Japan, the officer might have chased the boys and killed one of them.

This year, another son was born to Mr. Wu, and he was named Kunhua. He was seven years younger than the third son, Genghua. A wet nurse was hired to feed the baby. A crib was put in their bedroom. As there was not enough space, Genghua went to sleep with the grandma in her small room. They shared the same bed. The cot was moved to the third floor room for the wet nurse. The nurse had more milk than the baby needed, so she was told to squeeze out some milk into a bowl, which was given to Genghua as he was, indeed, of poor health as predicted by the fortune-teller.

When the Chinese army entered Shanghai, there was a parade to celebrate the victory, with a military band as always, and soldiers on horseback, in other words cavalry. A girl was sitting on a truck, dressed as goddess of victory.

Genghua suffered from typhoid that year and stopped going to school. A doctor came to see him at home and prescribed some medication. At first he lay in bed all day. The grandma would feed him with easily digested food. The tutor no longer came as the third son was sick and the second son did not want to study. Later, Genghua read books by himself with the help of dictionaries. Two Chinese dictionaries were commonly used at that time: "Source of Vocabulary" and "Sea of Vocabulary." And every day of an evening, he would listen to story-telling programs on the radio. Later in the evening the radio would be taken to the father's bedroom as he liked to listen to his favorite programs at night. One program was ghost-story telling round midnight. When Genghua slept in the big bedroom, he listened to this program, too. Some children were afraid of ghosts even when listening to a story of them. But not Genghua — especially with adults in the same room. One story was about a corpse turning into a vampire. Vampires in Chinese stories are different from those described in the US. The Chinese vampire could only jump stiffly after people. When a vampire caught someone, it would strangle the person to death. It was said that when a vampire killed a person, he would take the incarnation to be born as a living human.

One story about a vampire went like this: Four people were sitting up all night playing mahjong and keeping an eye on the body of a family member who was laid on a wooden plank. In some Chinese villages, when a person died and his body was laid out, family members or relatives had to sit in the same room to watch over it lest wild animals attack the corpse. This time, as the four people sat round a table playing mahjong through the night, the corpse became a vampire and sat up. The person facing the body saw it, but he didn't give a warning. He just stood up saying that he would go to the bathroom. When he left, two other people gave a yawn and turned about. Seeing the vampire sit up, they followed suit with the same excuse. The last person was sitting with his back toward the body and didn't see anything. Then the vampire got to its feet and jumped over. It made some noise and the last person turned round and saw it. He dashed to the corner of the room with a broom there. He took it up and threw it at the vampire. The vampire could not see anything. It just acted by vampire's instinct. It caught the broom in its hands and strangled it. So the fourth person escaped, too.

There were two programs in succession that told famous stories known to almost all Chinese people. The first was the *Legend of White Snake*, and the second was called *Smile Thrice*. The white snake was a thousand years old and achieved a magic power. She lived in a mountain, practicing her magic power under the moonlight. In the same mountain there lived a green snake who was five hundred years old and also had magic power. But the magic power of the white snake was stronger than that of the green snake. So when they fought for the dominance of the mountain, the green snake failed and became subjected to the white snake. One day the white snake transformed herself into a beautiful girl in a white dress and the green snake into a girl, too, as her maid, in a green dress. They went to the human world to enjoy life there. Then the white snake met a young man on West Lake in Hangzhou. She loved the man and summoned a shower. The young man ran for shelter. She produced an umbrella by magic power and shared it with the young man, who fell in love with the pretty girl at first sight — as in most love stories. Then they got married. A monk, who had magic power too, thought it not right for a snake to marry a mortal and meddled with their life. Once he kidnapped the young man and took him to the temple he lived in. When the white snake found out, she and the green snake went there to fight the monk. But the monk was more powerful. The two snakes had to retreat.

As the monk could foretell things, he knew that it was not the right time yet to deal the white snake a final blow. So he let the young man go back to the white snake. The young man went back to Hangzhou and met his snake wife on the Broken Bridge on a dike of the West Lake. "Meeting on the Broken Bridge" was a well-known scene or episode in the story. Then the white snake got pregnant and gave birth to a son. After the son was born to her, the monk thought it was time to punish the white snake for her marrying a mortal. So he came to Hangzhou again and got the snake in his magic jar and buried her under a pagoda, called Thunder-Peak Pagoda, which is a famous scenic spot in Hangzhou. When the son grew up and learned what had happened, he went to the pagoda and knelt before it, crying so bitterly that the Jade King in Heaven was touched, and the pagoda collapsed and the snake released. And the pagoda really did collapse, but the reason was not for the crying of the son. And of course, there was no snake under it. It was said that inside the bricks, with which the pagoda was built, there were valuable Buddhist sutra paper. So people went there to dig bricks out for the sutra paper. The bricks were taken by degrees till the loss of bricks reached the point that the rest of the bricks could not support the weight of the pagoda any more, and the pagoda crumbled.

Another version of the story was that when the white snake was put under the pagoda, the green snake escaped to hide in the mountain. She exercised her magic power to make it stronger and stronger till one day her power got strong enough to go against the monk. She went to fight the monk and released the white snake. But the original version is one handed down and more consistent with traditional tales. The second is a modern revised version.

The story of Smile Thrice was about a famous scholar in the Ming Dynasty, Tang Yin by name, who lived in Suzhou. Suzhou was the capital of the Wu kingdom thousands of years ago. The wife of King Wu was Xishi, a renowned beauty. She was the first one of the four beauties in the Chinese history. The second one was Wang Zhaojun of West Han Dynasty, who was sent to marry the chieftain of a minority in the north for the aim of keeping peace between the two nations as the minority often invaded the Han Dynasty. The third one was Diaochan of East Han Dynasty, who used her beauty as a stratagem to cause fighting between the father, an evil courtier, and the adopted son, who killed the father to get the beauty as his wife, ridding the country of an evil man. The last beauty was Yang Yuhuan, an imperial concubine of the emperor of Tang Dynasty, whose brother became the prime minister. His flawed administration of national affairs brought the country to chaos and revolt. When the revolting army approached the capital, the emperor had to escape west, taking his concubine. The prime minister followed him. Not far from the capital, his angry bodyguards refused to advance. They killed the prime minister as he was responsible for the bad situation, and moreover, forced the emperor to let his concubine die. The fourth beauty thus ended her life.

The first beauty, Xishi, had been a village girl in the Yue kingdom. When the Yue kingdom was defeated by the Wu kingdom, King Yue wanted to revenge. His tactic was to find a beautiful girl to send to King Wu. One day the village girl was found by one of his courtiers while she was washing her clothes in a stream. She was taken to the palace of King Yue and was trained in singing and dancing, and sent to King Wu, who loved her so much he neglected his national affairs. King Yue secretly trained new soldiers and made weapons. When he was strong enough, he conquered King Wu at last. In one version of the story, a courtier of King Yue then took away the dazzling beauty and hid her somewhere lest King Yue should also be a victim to her beauty and make his country perish, too. There are many reminders of the beauty Xishi in Suzhou.

Now back to the story of the scholar, Tang Yin, whose paintings are highly prized nowadays. The tale is imaginary. It goes like this: One day, he went to a famous temple outside Suzhou City to worship the Buddha and by chance saw a beautiful girl there. The girl was a handmaiden in the family of a high-ranking official, whose big residence was situated outside Wuxi City, also a renowned place for travelers. An old lady, the wife of the official, came to the temple to worship the Buddha, too. The handmaiden accompanied the old lady there. They had come by ship. When the lovely young woman knelt on a long mat, kowtowing to the Buddha, Tang went down on his knees by her on the same mat, which was long enough for three people to kneel on it simultaneously, and purposely set one of his knees on a corner of her skirt. When she wanted to get up, she had to say "Excuse me!" with a forced smile (the first smile). Tang excused himself and got to his feet.

Then he followed the girl wherever she went with the old lady till they got aboard on their ship. Tang knew that they would soon leave. He hurried to take a boat to follow the ship wherever it went. It would take several days to reach the residence. Next morning when he stood on the bow of the boat, enjoying the sights around, the handmaiden came out from the main cabin, carrying a basin of water in which the old lady had washed her face and hands. She stood in the stern of the ship and poured the water from the basin into the river, without noticing that there was a boat right behind them. The water went all over Tang, who cried out wrathfully. But as he saw that it was the girl who had done it, he forgot the whole unhappy thing and smiled to her. She smiled back (second smile) as if to say she was sorry. After three days the ship reached its destination. The old lady and the girl stepped ashore and so did Tang. When the girl beheld the man again, she did not know what to think. She noted that the man kept staring at her, and she just smiled goodbye to him (third smile). The girl's here smiles hit Tang with various kinds of whimsical fancies. He took the smiles as a sign of love. Therefore, Tang sold himself under a false name to the family as a servant. The old couple had two sons who were dim witted. They could barely write a simple composition. As Tang once displayed his skills in writing, the father let him teach his sons. So he did not need to do any servants' work. The funny thing was that the wife of the second son was his cousin. He managed to avoid being seen by her, or his real identification would be known. Even so, the cousin came to know who was the new servant, but she did not reveal the secret. She only demanded that Tang create a painting for her, and Tang could not refuse for fear of being given away. Generally Tang did not paint as a favor. He only painted when inspiration urged him, or for money. The cousin had not got a painting from him as a memento yet. At that time, rich people deemed it an honor to have a painting by Tang hanging on the wall of their living rooms so that guests could see the painting.

Then he got a chance to meet the girl alone. He revealed his true identity to her, and she started to love the famous painter. Finally he eloped with her and they lived happily together till silvery threads came into their hair.

Genghua gradually regained his health. He did not need to lie in bed all day long. He got up and moved around in the house, and then he was allowed to play with other boys in the neighborhood. Games boys played at that time were top-whipping, shooting marbles, leapfrog, mini-football, shuttlecock-kicking, and cards, etc. The glass marbles were played like this: boys found a space somewhere in the lane and drew a small square on the ground with chalk, then drew a line some distance away from the square. Every boy joining in the game put a glass marble in the square. Boys stood at the line and played by turns. One of them took out another marble from his pocket and shot it at the marbles in the square. If he could hit any marble and knock it out of the square, he won this marble. If the first boy did not hit any marbles in the square, another boy would shoot his marble in turn. When no more marbles were left, the game was over. They could start from the beginning, if they wanted to continue. Boys played cards not like adults in gambling. They put up two cards one end against each other with the other end apart on the ground, forming something looking like a tent. One boy threw a card at the card tent from some distance and tried to knock it down. If he knocked it down, he could have the two cards. If he failed, another boy took over his place. Whoever got most cards was the final winner. Boys seldom played rope-jumping unless some girls invited the boy to join, who had nothing better to do and just stood aside, watching. Boys had another game called running and catching. One boy stood apart from other boys acting as the catcher. Other boys stood with the body against a wall or touched hands on the wall. If anyone or more than one boys ran off the wall, the catcher could go after him or one of them. If the catcher touched his hand on any boy, the boy had to change positions with the catcher and acted as next catcher. The former catcher went to the wall. The game started anew. Boys often played with a little ball, a little smaller than the baseball in size. At both ends of a space they put two things apart, whatever they were, as goals. They could be two bricks standing on end, or two satchels when the boys played it after school. Sometimes Genghua joined in the game. On such an occasion, he would put on a pair of leather shoes, as their tips were harder than those of the cloth shoes that he wore most of the time during the day. Cloth shoes were soft and comfortable. But with his leather shoes, the other boys were afraid to contend with Genghua for the possession of the ball lest their feet should be hurt if Genghua kicked their feet with the hard tips by accident. Genghua took this advantage consciously. That was why he always changed shoes when he wanted to play the ball game.

Big boys liked to play Chinese yoyo, which uses a short round wooden stick with two round disks, 1.5 cm thick with a space between them, attached on either end of the stick. The disk has small openings on the side. It will rotate on a string, each end tied to a thin stick. The player holds the two thin sticks in his hands and swing the string right and left, with the yoyo on the string. When played hard, the yoyo will give out a sharp shrill sound. At that time the yoyo was played in the winter, especially during the period of festivals. The shrill sound would add an exciting atmosphere to the festivals. A skillful player can use a pot cover as yoyo. Only the pot cover should have a round handle on it. The pot cover cannot make any sound. A player can throw the yoyo up in the air and catch it on the string when it falls, and continue to play.

Chapter 3 – How the Chinese Kept Their Festivals before 1949

At the corner of next block there was a marketplace with many small shops. Some shops sold clothes, shoes, toys, or food and drink. One shop that was popular with men and big boys was a game shop where one could shoot a popgun at marks lined up on the inner-most side of the shop. There was a tiny hole on every mark. If a pellet was shot into the hole, the mark was hit. One mark was an eagle hung on a string. When hit, it would slide down the string to the bottom. The most popular mark was a girl wearing a dress. When it was hit, the dress would fall aside revealing the girl naked.

One shop was a book rental, with everything from picture books to classics. Genghua often went there to rent books. He loved to read. He was intellectually precocious, and rented books such as Three Kingdoms, The Beach, and Journey to West, at the age of nine. He would put a low footstool outside the door near the wall and sit on it with his back against the wall, reading the books he had rented, because the illumination outside was better than inside under a lamp. Some teenagers would hide one book inside their jackets and take two books to the counter for checking out. The owner could not see what they had done, and so they paid only for two books, but read three. When they returned the two books, they secretly put the third one back onto the shelves where it belonged. Since no book was missing, the owner did not seem to take notice of this practice. Anyway, it did not work in summer as the boys had no jackets.

The second son, Dinghua, was strong and naughty, and sometimes fought with other boys. Some boys liked to shoot at each other, using a slingshot, while hiding behind walls or other cover. Some boys shot paper pellets from the windows of their houses at the boys walking past in the lane. When the boys being hit looked up, they pretended to know nothing about it. Waste paper was folded up tight to make the pellets, and a rubber band could be used to shoot it. Sometimes when he had nothing better to do, Genghua would make such pellets for his stepbrother. He himself did not like to fight.

If Mr. Wu found out that his second son did anything wrong, he would beat his palm with a ruler or have him kneel before the narrow, long table in the corner of the living room farthest to the door, on which Mr. Wu kept a Buddha statuette. He burned incense and candles on the first day and the fifteenth day of every moon. And he would chant some Buddhist sutras for half an hour, counting the beads on a string at the same time. When the second son knelt before the Buddha, Mr. Wu would burn a joss stick and put it in the burner. The son could only get up when the joss stick burned to the end. It generally took one hour. If the offense was not serious, the new wife would beg the husband to pardon him. Then the second son would be grateful to her. Doings of a wise person.

The most exciting days for children were the eve and the first day of the lunar year, or Spring Festival; the fifteenth day of the first moon, or Lantern Festival, and the fifteenth day of the eighth moon, or Mid-Autumn Festival. Three major festivals in the lunar year. On the eve of the lunar new year, the Wu family used to worship their ancestors. In the living room, a square table was put in the middle with six chairs, two at one side, and the side without chairs was left open for family members to worship. Before the table on this side there was a kneeling mat for members to kneel on and kowtow three times to the ghosts of their ancestors sitting on the chairs, one after another, in age sequence. On the table there was a burner for joss sticks with two candles on either side of it. Candles and incense were burning. There were nine hot dishes on the table with six pairs of chopsticks, six cups of wine, each before one chair. Supposedly, the ghosts of the ancestors would come to enjoy the worshiping of the descendants. As the ghosts could not actually eat anything, they were presumed to inhale the aromatic steam from the hot dishes. Toward the end of the ritual, paper money would be burned, for the ghosts to use in the other world. When the dishes turned cold, the ghosts were presumed to have left and the ceremony was over. Then the incense burner and candlesticks were removed to the long table in the corner. The dishes were carried to the kitchen to be reheated. Then the square table was set for the family members to dine. After dinner they would light fireworks and firecrackers and what we today call bottle rockets, all popping and shooting skyward and exploding with smoke and sparks.

Big boys liked to play with a special kind of fireworks which was made by putting gunpowder in a clay ball. When the clay ball was cast on the ground or a wall, it would explode and bits of clay would fly. Once Mr. Wu's second son threw a clay ball on the ground just as a woman walked by. Her silk stockings were burned with a tiny hole. Mrs. Wu came out and paid the lady for it. The second son was nowhere to be seen. Mrs. Wu did not tell her husband about it.

For the eve of the lunar new year, adults would sit up for the night while children had to sleep. Next day was the lunar New Year's Day. When children woke up, they would find a small red envelope under the pillow, containing some New Year money. This is the tradition for thousands of years. The children got up and put on new clothes, specially made for the New Year. Then children would get on their knees to kowtow to their parents and other elders. Instead of saying Happy New Year, they would say "make a fortune" (in the New Year). Breakfast for that day had to be something sweet, which meant that the new year would begin with happiness. Later, guests would come to greet the family, or the head of the family would go out to his friends' houses for the same purpose. When elder guests came, the children had to kowtow to them, and they in turn gave a red envelope to each of the children as New Year money. A servant would bring in a cup of tea for a guest, who in turn would put another red envelope with money under the cup. After the guest left and a servant took the cup away, the mistress of the house would collect the envelopes and put them in a box. A friend of Mr. Wu's, Mr. Rong Meixin, often put two American dollars in the envelopes. After the festival was over, the mistress of the house would divide the money among all the servants. As for the money for the children, the parents would say that the money would be saved in the bank and used for their tuition.

For many days, friends would gather every evening in the house of a common friend or in a restaurant. Some would go to a whore-house for the dinner there, but it was not necessarily what you think. A bawd would always welcome such patrons. After dinner, the patrons would generally return home. Don't think that men always had sex with whores in the whorehouse. Most businessmen went there to have dinner while talking about business. Meanwhile, they let the bawd have some money.

Such activities would last till after the lantern festival, which would begin on the thirteenth day of the first moon and last till the eighteenth day. The fifteenth day was the climax for the celebration. Lanterns of various shapes were for sale in many shops. The favorite lantern for children was the lantern framed as a rabbit with a small candle lit inside. Colored paper would be stuck around the frame with four tiny wheels attached so that it could be pulled along. Of course, these rabbit lanterns sometimes tipped over as a child was pulling it, and paper would catch fire and lantern burn away. Then a child might cry. The mother would cajole it by promising to buy another one someday.

On the evening of the fifteenth day, most families would have small round dumplings with various stuffings, some sweet with sesame and sugar and some salty with meatballs. That day was Genghua's birthday. By Chinese tradition, children's birthday was not celebrated every year. No cake at that time for the occasion. The best thing was the eating of a bowl of noodles with a fried chop and some spinach on it, or two big shrimps with long antennae stretching forward. Only on the tenth birthday there would be a party and gifts. Genghua's tenth birthday was celebrated at home. The square table in the living room could only seat eight people, so a big round wooden top was put on the square table so that it became a round table for twelve people. The board could be folded and stored under the staircase. Some of Genghua's schoolmates and some playmates in the neighborhood were invited. No candles were needed since there was no birthday cake. It was like a dinner party. The young guests were treated with hot dishes and bowls of noodle at the end. No birthday song was sung. Nothing of that kind: that is the Western way of celebrating a birthday. Genghua's parents adhered to the old Chinese style. Anyway, birthday gifts were given: some toys and books. A friend of his father's presented to him with a subscription to a magazine, one issue every month. Genghua liked it very much. One story was so moving that Genghua could never forget it.

The story told about a small, pretty girl who was apt to laugh at other girls for whatever they did wrong, or even for a natural bodily deformation. Once she told her mother that she had a classmate who had a pockmarked face, and she often laughed at her for that. Her mother told her that she should not laugh at disfigured people. But the girl would not listen. One day, the girl suffered from a pox herself, and after she recovered, her own face turned out to be pockmarked. She cried bitterly. The mother consoled her, saying "When you laugh at other people for their deformation, you can also get such deformation some day. From this you have learned a lesson." From then on, the girl never laughed at other people.

For Mid-Autumn Festival, Chinese people eat moon cakes. The origin of this was a legend. When China was ruled by a minority tribe from the north, people wanted to revolt and drove them back to where they came from. People wanted to rise to arms on the same day, the fifteenth day of the eighth moon. So they made moon cakes, stuffing a slip of paper with such message on it inside the moon cakes. When other people got the moon cakes and eat them, they got the message. Hence, people of later generations kept the tradition of eating moon cakes. There are a few different sorts of moon cakes in China. One sort is made in Canton, the flour skin of it is baked brown with various stuffings inside, which can be sesame, walnut meat, pork, and the smashed lotus seeds with an egg yolk in the middle, the most welcome sort. All are sweetened. Another sort is invented in Suzhou, the skin of which is multi-layered, very thin layer, with stuffings of sesame, walnut meat, smashed date meat, etc. This sort of moon cakes are sweetened, too. Then the third sort appeared, the stuffing of which is minced pork meat inside multi-layered skin, not baked but fried brown, tasting salty.

On that day, besides eating moon cakes, people in the south of China also cook a duck soup. In the north, especially in Beijing, ducks are roasted, but in Shanghai, ducks are cooked in several ways. It can be cooked in soy sauce, or fried brown, then stuffed with rice and vegetables, and then steamed. Duck soup for that festival is cooked with taros.

These are the major festivals. There are some minor festivals such as Tomb-Sweeping Day in April, always falling on the Fifth Solar Term day, on which people go visiting the tombs of their kin. Generally in the olden times, they took incense, candles, and paper money to burn there, with some food or fruit put before the tombs. After a ceremony, the dishes and fruits were taken back. But nowadays, people just bring flowers and perhaps burn paper money.

Dragon Boat Festival is always on the fifth day of the fifth moon, on which there is a dragon boat competition. This tradition came from a historical story about a man named Qu Yuan, a courtier in Chu Kingdom in the War Period among Seven Kingdoms between the fifth century and the third century BC. At the end of that period, the Qin Kingdom became the strongest one among the seven kingdoms. The Chu Kingdom would soon be subdued. The courtier Qu Yuan did not want to witness the Qin army marching into his motherland, and so he drowned himself in a river by holding a heavy stone in his arms. People in later dynasties honored his devotion and rowed boats to show a desire to retrieve his body from the water for suitable burial. Hence, the tradition. People also cast sticky rice wrapped in bamboo leaves (zongzi, it is called) in the water in the hope that the fish and other water creatures would not eat his body, but eat the zongzi instead. So another tradition Chinese people keep on that day is to eat zongzi. The third tradition at that time was that people drank wine with realgar (an arsenic ore) in it to keep off germs and small poisonous creatures. Adults would draw the Chinese character WANG on the forehead of children for the same reason. Moxa and calamus plants were hung at every doorframe for the purpose to drive away evil spirits. The last two traditions are no longer exercised.

One more thing about the Qin Dynasty. The king of Qin conquered the other six kingdoms and merged them into a huge empire, the first empire in Chinese history. The king made himself the first emperor of China, Emperor Qin. While he established China as a great nation, he was a bit of a tyrant and was famous for having many scholars buried alive and many books burned. He had the Great Wall built to defend the realm, but in lots of workers died building it. So people of that time hated him and people of the later dynasties criticized him. However, Chairman Mao of the Chinese Communist Party worshiped him and imitated him too many ways. He defended China from foreign invasion and foreign interference, but he persecuted his contemporary intellectuals and caused millions of Chinese people to die in shifting political movements and the years of needless famine.

Another festival is on the seventh day of the seventh moon, on which day the Cowboy and the Girl Weaver would meet on a heavenly river. It comes from a story, which goes like this: A daughter of the heavenly mother comes to the human world. She meets a cowboy and falls in love with him, but the heavenly mother forbids her to marry a mortal and forces her to go back to heaven. Only after daughter begs her and pleads with her, the heavenly mother permits her to meet the cowboy once a year on the seventh day of the seventh moon. But to meet her, the cowboy had to cross the heavenly river (what Westerners call the Milky Way). Since he cannot do that, he cries on the bank. Just then, a huge group of magpies fly up to form a bridge, which Chinese people call Magpie Bridge. The cowboy goes over the Magpie Bridge and meet the daughter once every year.

Another tradition was for girls to try to thread a needle under the moonlight that night. If a girl could do it, she was certainly very skillful. But this tradition is no longer kept nowadays.

Another minor festival is on the ninth day of the ninth moon, the Double Ninth festival, when old people head for the top of the nearest hill or mountain. This tradition developed from a story, too. The story goes back to the East Han Dynasty when a god by the name of Fei Changfang said to his disciple Huanjing that on the ninth day of the ninth moon, the river monster would bring a plague to his family. If he made certain preparations and took his family to the top of a nearby hill, he could elude it. The man did as he was told. When he and his family returned home that evening, all the livestock had been killed. If the family had been at home, they would have died as well. In the later dynasties, climbing to a hilltop was deemed good exercise or a pleasurable outing.

Chapter 4 – Life of the Wu Family before the Communist Party takes over Shanghai

Business was good for Mr. Wu after the victory. Many of his friends bought cars or minivans from abroad. Mr. Wu bought a beige-colored De Soto car and hired a chauffeur who lived with the family. He slept on a camp cot in the living room. The manservant left to work in a factory and the woman servant left to work in a textile factory, both on the recommendation of Mr. Wu. Another older woman came from Ningpo to work for the family as a cook; her feet were small and deformed, having been bound in her child-hood. The back of the foot looked like a hunch and the shape of the sole was somewhat like a triangle with the big toe as the top angle. The four small toes were a little tucked in toward the sole. When she was a little child, her feet were bound tight with cloth to pre-vent them from growing normally big, and the lower leg was kept abnormally thin. This custom went back to the reign of Emperor Li Yi (937–978 AD) of the South Tang Dynasty during the period of Six Dynasties. No record shows how the tradition really began, but having tiny feet was a sign of a lady, not a common peasant. Farming women, who had to work in the fields, had to have strong legs and feet. The tradition was officially abolished only upon the overthrow of the Qing Dynasty in 1911.

Mr. Wu also bought a Westinghouse refrigerator to replace the old ice box, the same as ice boxes that were used elsewhere, which relied on large blocks of ice to keep the contents cool. A container underneath would catch water as the ice melted.

Wealth can encourage people to live less disciplined lives. Having the luxury of free time allowed Mr. Wu to develop a hobby of playing mahjong. He often had friends over and his new wife cooked delicious food for them. And sometimes, Mr. Wu would go to some of his friends' houses.

Sometimes the friends would go to a whorehouse to play mahjong and for other entertainment. As noted earlier, this was a general house of entertainment, as the cook was very good and made some special dishes, and some of the girls were good singers and could sing some pieces of Peking opera beautifully. One of the men knew the madam, and they would go there just to let her earn some money. Generally after dinner they stopped playing and went home.

His sons liked it when their father sat down to play mahjong, whether somewhere else or at home, because he was intent on playing and had no time to discipline his sons. They would go out to find their respective playmates. If it was raining and his father was at home, Genghua liked to take shelter in the car, where he had a special feeling of being in a space all his own.

The fourth son was now two years old, but still could not speak. They asked him if he was mute, and he would shake his head "no." He began to speak at four! When Mr. Wu was at home, the chauffeur would pick up the child and take Genghua somewhere to enjoy some free time, leaving a message with the grandma about where they were going. It was a good excuse for the chauffeur if his boss wanted him and could not find him. To take children for a ride would certainly please the parents and who could scold him for that?

Sometimes they went to "Big World," which had three storeys round a central space, mostly stages for all kinds of performances such as magicians' shows, plays, acrobatics, story-telling, cross-talks, and all sorts of operas: Peking opera, Shanghai opera, Shaoxing opera. There were a lot of booths in the central space, selling food. Just inside the entrance there was a hall of mirrors, all distorted, some concave, some convex, some like the curved part of a bow. They were called Ha-Ha-Mirrors. People could stay in there for the whole day, especially those who had come to Shanghai for the first time from deep in the countryside or from other cities. Once when the chauffeur went there with the sons, he bent down in a low crouch, carrying the child in his arms and telling Genghua to follow him closely. He and the children hid among the crowds and moved together with them. Since they stayed so low, the ticket collector could not see them among the crowds so that they got in for free.

The Wu family kept a white cat and a black dog. The white cat had followed the grandma home and so stayed with the family ever since. The dog was given by a friend, a house-warming gift. In a Chinese myth, the god of fortune rides on a black tiger. The black dog was symbolic of the black tiger, which meant that Mr. Wu would make a great fortune. The family also had two hens for laying eggs and a duck, all kept in a wicker crate under the table in the kitchen. In the daytime, they were let out to move about outside the house. Once it was raining hard and water flooded the lane. As the house was on a high foundation, water did not enter the house. The duck was let out and it happily swam on the water. When the rain stopped, the street was still flooded, so a man next door tied two small stools on his feet and walked in the water like on stilts.

Granny liked to feed the cat and the dog. She fed the cat rice in fish soup, covered with the fish head and tail, and the dog with rice in beef soup, covered with some beef bits.

In summer, the boys liked to drink cold soda water directly from the bottle. They could not drink fast as the mouth of the bottle was small. They thought that no one could drink fast from the bottle. Once they bet with the chauffeur if he could finish a big bottle of soda water in a minute. If he failed, he should buy them some candy. But they forgot to add the condition that he had to drink directly from the bottle. The chauffeur opened the bottle, poured the soda water into a glass, and drank it from the glass very fast. He finished it within a minute. The boys had not thought of doing it this way. Boys are boys, innocent and inexperienced.

In spring, 1947, Genghua was found to have tuberculosis. The doctor gave him an injection the color of milk. TB sufferers need to breathe fresh air, so the father took him to Hangzhou on a tour in April, the season for sightseeing. The new wife was left home to take care of the household. Hangzhou is famous for West Lake. They went with a group of friends and their family. They rented a bus to drive them there and round the city, and then back. The bus started in the morning and arrived in Hangzhou in the evening. The bus stopped at the foot of a mountain. The tourists ascended to the top and lodged in the taoist temple there for the night. There were guest rooms in the back of the temple. After a simple supper, some ladies were playing mahjong in a guest room. Someone had remembered to bring a mahjong set. A bit later, Genghua and the children of other families went to the main hall where there was a taoist ritual going on. A long table stood in the center, the chief taoist behind it, other taoists on either side of it; all were chanting something from a taoist sutra. The chief taoist looked like he was dancing with a wooden sword in his right hand. At the end of the ceremony the chief taoist took a yellow piece of paper from the table with some signs drawn on it. The wooden sword had a little split at the thin end, in which the chief taoist put the yellow paper. He held the paper to the candle fire and the paper began to burn. The taoist wielded the sword upward and the burning paper flew up in the air. Then the ashes gradually hovered down like butterflies onto the floor.

West Lake is divided by a long dike into two sections: inner lake and outer lake. At that time lotus leaves covered the surface of the inner lake. In summer, the lotus flowers would be in full bloom all over the water, spreading their faint perfume. They rented a boat. It carried the tourists everywhere they wanted to go around in the lake. They visited Yue Fei Temple on the northern shore. Yue Fei was a general in the South Song Dynasty who insisted on resisting an invasion by the Jin tribe from the north. But some courtiers wanted to negotiate with Jin tribe rather than fight the tribe to the last ditch. So those courtiers gave orders to summon him to the capital, and there they murdered him. But people looked upon him as a national hero. In later dynasties, people worshiped him as a god and set up a temple for him. In the back of the temple was his tomb. On either side of his tomb there were four cast iron statues in kneeling posture, who were those courtiers who had killed him. There was a famous couplet inscribed on either side of the door frame facing the tomb. It reads:

> *The green mountain is so lucky with loyal bones buried under;*
> *The white iron is so innocent, being cast into statues of traitors.*

Many people maintained that it was unwise of Yue Fei to go back to the capital to be killed in jail. There is a principle in the military classic "Art of War," by Sun Tzu, that when a commander is far away from the emperor, on the battlefield, he should use his discretion and not necessarily obey orders from the emperor. The situation on the battlefield is changeable and any order from the emperor in the far off capital may not be suitable under the actual fighting conditions. So the commander has the right to refuse to follow. People wished he had just driven back the northern tribe and then gone to the capital to arrest those courtiers so that they would not further influence the emperor with decisions that ran against the nation's benefit.

Their second stop on the lake was an isle called the Three Ponds Mirroring the Moon. A little distance from the isle there are three metal sculptures shaped like big incense burners above the water. They form a triangle, and on the night of the fifteenth day of the eighth lunar month, the moon places its image in the center of the triangle.

In June that year, Mr. Wu went to visit a friend, Mr. Cheng, in the city of Suzhou, a tourist attraction. According to a Chinese saying, "Paradise is in heaven and Suzhou and Hangzhou are on earth." The friend had a son living and work in Hong Kong. Mr. Wu had given the son a letter of recommendation, with which he found a job. So the father was grateful to Mr. Wu. This time when the father and the son came to Suzhou, they lodged in the friend's house, which was a house of typically Chinese style. On entering the gate, there was a courtyard before a set of rooms under one roof, forming the first building, with a well in the courtyard. Behind this building, there was another courtyard connecting to another building, both with two storeys. Next morning for breakfast, they were served with a bowl of fresh Gordon Euryale (Euryale ferox) seeds cooked in sweet soup. The seeds were chewy and pleasant.

Horse-drawn carriages provided a kind of public transportation. The carriage had a running board on either side for the riders to use as a step when getting on and off. Once while the father and son were riding in such a carriage, a man jumped on the running board, holding a bowl of vinegar in one hand and grasping the side of the carriage with his other hand. Maybe he had just bought the vinegar and was going home. He got the free ride, and this kind of hitching a ride was common.

Before leaving Suzhou to return to Shanghai, Mr. Wu invited his friend to have lunch in the famous restaurant "Pine & Stork." They had a special dish of fried fish; the skin of the fish was fried crisp and had a sour sauce, while the fish meat was tender and delicious. Then Mr. Wu bought a few boxes of sweet sliced dried fruits to take back to Shanghai for his young wife.

Mr. Wu had another friend in Shanghai, Zhou Xiangsheng, who owned a big, famous taxi company. Its phone number was 40000, very easy to remember. Then he gave this company to his brother, Zhou Shanyuan, and he himself opened another taxi company, with the phone number 60000. During the Anti-Japanese War, he donated many military trucks to the government and after the victory he was given a title of major. Mr. Zhou gave Mr. Wu his picture in a frame wearing the major's uniform. The picture was nowhere to be seen when the Communist Party took over Shanghai. Lucky for Mr. Wu.

It was 1948. Mr. Wu's eldest son graduated from a university in Nanking and he joined the US air force as an interpreter. Before long, it seems he ran afoul of military discipline and was about to be taken into custody, but he ran off and no one knew where. The police came to the father's house to look for him, but of course he was not there. The police only found two US air force uniforms:

little ones, made for the boys, as many boys love to wear uniforms — any time in any country, whether permitted or not permitted by the law. And in the end, somehow, the eldest son made it to the United States and lived there ever since.

Genghua was in the fourth grade. He studied well and often got good marks. As far as marks were concerned, he and other two girls were always the top three. Sometimes he was the first and the two girls were the second and the third. Then one of the girls was the first and he and the other girl were the second and the third. There was an award for that. The first did not need to pay the tuition. The second only paid half of the tuition, and the third paid two-thirds, though the tuition was not high.

At that time, teachers could apply physical punishment if a student did something wrong or something the teacher thought wrong. The punishment was always that the teacher told the wrong-doer to come in front and hold out his or her hand. The teacher would use a ruler to hit the palm. Boys never cried for the pain, but girls might shed some tears. The teacher could not hurt the student severely, or the parents would complain. Genghua was a tame student and never got any punishment.

Mr. Wu's fourth son liked small model cars of any design, mostly made from tin plate. A few were made of celluloid. A jeep was of this kind. When it was pushed by the hand, it could run a long way before stopping. Once the chauffeur suggested to put a lit candle on its seat. When it moved, the candlelight flickered. It looked wonderful when the room was dark, the lights being turned off. But one day, when the chauffeur and the fourth son played with it like always, the lit candle fell and the celluloid jeep caught fire and was damaged.

In Shanghai at that time, almost every business had a guild to protect the benefits of the businessmen in the same trade. A director would be elected to take care of everything for the guild. Mr. Wu was elected the director as he was known as a good man among friends and colleagues. At the time, the political situation looked bad for the National Party (in Chinese this is the KuoMing [meaning National] Dang [meaning Party], or KMD. It was led by Chiang

Kai-shek, who was defeated by the Communist Party and escaped to Taiwan). Quite a few friends of Mr. Wu's moved to Hong Kong. Someone advised Mr. Wu to move there with them, but with his business in Shanghai, he did not see how he could relocate. At that time, Hong Kong was not so prosperous. Besides, the Communist Party was promising democracy and freedom to people then. For that reason, many businessmen and other people of property stayed in Shanghai, to their great regret afterwards. For many people this error cost them their lives.

The husband of the new wife's sister wanted to borrow money from Mr. Wu. Mr. Wu lent him two big gold bars and got an IOU in return. That was a clever man and he went to Hong Kong before the communist party came to Shanghai.

In May 1949, the roar of cannons was heard in the outskirts of Shanghai for a few days. But no battle was waged in the city. On the 27th day, the so-called Liberation Army marched into the city of Shanghai peacefully.

Chapter 5 – The Communist "Liberation Army" and the Korean War

People in Shanghai welcomed the Liberation Army like they had welcomed Chiang Kai-shek's army after the long occupation of Japan. But they were later disappointed in Chiang Kai-shek's government for corruption. So now they pinned their hopes on the Communist Party, while wondering whether if the Communist Party would disappoint them in new ways, or just be corrupt like Chiang Kai-shek's government.

At first, business and life went on more or less as usual. Genghua suffered again from tuberculosis and rested at home. Eventually an effective TB remedy, rimifoni, was invented, and the boy recovered. Then Mr. Wu decided to sell his house and rented another house on Central Fuxing Road. He sold the car as well, so the chauffeur left to find a job as a bus driver. The maidservant Ahmei married a self-employed tailor. Only the old woman went with the family. The whole family lived in the new house.

People were not allowed to keep livestock in the city any more. So hens and the duck were killed and cooked. The cat had died. The dog went with them to the new home, but one day he dog ran out of the house and bit a boy next door. Not wishing to risk any trouble,

Mr. Wu gave the dog away. Now Mr. Wu had to go everywhere by riding in a pedicab. At that time pedicabs were main public transportation. Empty pedicabs, just like taxis, roamed in the street for passengers. Anyone could beckon to the driver, and he would take the passenger anywhere he wanted to go at a price they both agreed.

The rented house was of the single room type with three storeys, a big room on every floor, with a small mezzanine room between the second and third floors. Grandma slept in there. The other small mezzanine room between the ground and the second floors was originally designed to be the bathroom. The ground floor was still used as living room. There was a space under the staircase, in which a camp cot was put up for the woman to sleep at night. The parents slept on the second floor with the fourth son on a cot in their room. As for the third floor room, half of it was partitioned as a storeroom and Genghua slept in the other half, and later the auntie, the sister of the wife, moved in to share the space with Genghua. Another bed was added. The auntie had been deserted by her husband, who went to Hong Kong alone. So she had to come to live with her sister. As the first son had gone to the US, the second son moved back to live with his mother.

Sometimes a siren would sound, announcing an air raid. Bombers were sent by the Chiang Kai-shek government to make a disturbance in Shanghai. The local government issued orders to stick thin strips of paper across every window pane so that if the glass were broken by an explosion, broken glass would not fly all over. But Genghua never heard of any serious damage anywhere in Shanghai due to air raids. Maybe the bombers never dropped any bombs.

Genghua found a peculiar thing in the neighborhood. One day he was walking in the street just outside his lane, and he saw a dog holding a basket in its mouth. He went into a small variety shop. The owner of the shop took the money from the basket and put in a pack of cigarettes and some change. The dog took the basket back to his master, a man living across the street. The man took the basket and gave the dog a little treat. Genghua asked the man how he did it, and he admitted that he'd had to "train" the neighbors as well as the dog, of course. The dog would buy his own food this way. Very funny.

In July of 1950, Mr. and Mrs. Wu went to Hangzhou with Genghua. They stayed in a hotel just on the south shore of the West Lake. They could look at the lake from the window of their room, enjoying the restful panorama of the West Lake with green hills in the background. Early in the morning, they strolled on the dike, breathing fresh air and enjoying the scenery. One day at noon they visited the place literally called "Watching-Fish-by-Flower-Bay." The sun was at the zenith and reflected in the center of the lake. The rippling water looked like golden scales of a fish. They got a table outside a tearoom under a pine tree. Breezes came from the lake, bringing coolness. Genghua was suddenly inspired to write a poem:

> *The lovely sun falls in the center of the lake, being enervated (?),*
> *Splashing with golden specks in the clear waves.*
> *I love the distant hills, now bright, now dim, as I linger,*
> *Treasuring alone the cool shade under the pine tree.*

Next day they took bus to Hidden Deity Temple. The name was derived from a legend. In the Song Dynasty, there was a monk called Jigong in this temple. He was really an Arhan in disguise. In Buddhism, an Arhan is a kind of deity, living with Buddha Sakyamuni in the west. When Chinese people talk about the place Buddha Sakyamuni lives, they often refer to it as the western paradise because India is in the west to China. Monk Jigong always did something to benefit people or to punish evil persons. There is a book written about all his escapades, imaginary, of course. An interesting story goes like this: the son of the prime minister loved to watch cricket fight and kept some big crickets that could fight fiercely. The cricket fight was involved in bets on big money. One of his crickets was always victorious and so he treasured it. A servant was assigned to take care of the crickets for him. Every cricket was kept in an earthen container with a lid. One day the servant was feeding all the crickets one by one. The favorite cricket of the son, when the lid was lifted, jumped out of the container and was nowhere to be found. The son learned it and wanted to kill the servant for his neglect. Then Monk Jigong came to his rescue. He produced a big strong cricket out of nowhere. The son loved it at the first sight.

For next several days, he always won in the cricket fight. But one day when he himself opened the lid, this cricket jumped out and was soon nowhere to be found. This time, he could not punish the servant since it was his own fault for losing the treasured cricket.

There was a famous restaurant called "Heaven Beyond Heaven" before the temple. The Wu family had lunch there. The dishes offered included shrimps eaten alive, which were put on a plate covered with a big bowl. When one wanted to eat, he lifted the bowl a little, put in his chopsticks quickly under the bowl, snatched a living shrimp out, and let the bowl cover the plate again, or the live shrimps would jump out. Another dish was fish cooked in vinegar. The way of cooking it was to dip the clean fish into the pot with boiling water and let it stay there for a few minutes, then taken out and laid on a plate. The vinegar sauce was poured on it. The fish meat was very tender. After lunch, they went to see the temple.

They entered the temple and worshiped Buddha first in the main hall. Then they walked round the building to the back. There was a small knoll literally called "Fly-Here Knoll" beyond a clear creek. A small bridge spanned over it. A legend said that this small knoll had flown here from India because someone came from India, and when seeing it, said that there was a similar knoll in India and it might fly here. Hence, the name. Thick woods covered the knoll and at its foot there was a cave, inside which the air was very cool in summer. A few people lay on bamboo mattress they brought to escape from the heat outside. The trio sat at a table sipping tea while watching the knoll and the brook.

One night, they rented a boat and rowed it on the West Lake. The water surface was as smooth as a mirror. The moon cut its image in the depth of the lake. When breezes arose, the water rippled and the moon image in the water swayed with the ripples. The distant peaks were bright under the moonlight and the vales looked dark. Lamplights everywhere glowed like stars. The nocturnal view on the West Lake was so beautiful. When bells sounded somewhere in a temple, they returned to their hotel. They stayed for a week and back to Shanghai.

That year, the first movement of the Communist Party in China commenced in the countryside, dividing the tilling land belonging to landlords among peasants. On the 30th of June, 1950, the central people's government issued the "Land Reform Law of the People's Republic of China." Many Party cadres formed work teams and went to the countryside to instruct peasants how to do the job. The landlords were pulled out of their residences to an open space. They knelt on the ground. Some peasants who hated their landlords went forth to slap their faces. Many of them were shot to death. Even their families were deprived of their properties, leaving them only with necessities for life. Peasants moved into the houses of the land-lords. It was called land reform movement.

A funny story was that: a young man was the son of a land-lord. When his father died, he inherited a large stretch of land and became a landlord. He loved to gamble and in the end lost all his properties on the gaming table. He became a poor man. When the Communist Party came and the land reform movement began, he was safe and no one beat him as he was no longer a landlord. But the man who got all his land was deemed a landlord and was killed. Fate played jokes on humans.

Statistics showed that in 2,742 villages in the south of Jiangsu Province, beatings happened in 200 villages; 218 individual land-lords were punished by beating, being hung up, forced to kneel, stripped of clothes. In HeNan Province, over forty landlords were killed in one month. In Guangdong Province, at first, the movement went slowly and peacefully. Mao was dissatisfied and in February, 1952, Mao instructed that the movement be carried out faster. So a slogan went round in that province: "Blood must flow in every village. Every landlord family must be beaten." Accordingly, in the western part of that province 1,156 persons committed suicide or were beaten to death. At the beginning of the movement, some Par-ty leaders proposed a peaceful reform, but Mao persisted in violent reform. He never was disturbed that people were dying as he im-posed his theory of class struggle. But he himself treasured his own life. Legend has it that in his early revolutionary life, he was once caught by a soldier when he was running away. The soldier did not know who he was. Mao bribed him, and so he let Mao go.

The second movement was to arrest so-called reactionaries. Who were the "reactionaries"? It's hard to define. The movement began in December, 1950, and ended in October, 1951. Three million people were caught up in it, and many innocent people were arrested and even executed. People were easily executed without proper legal procedure, maybe with nothing more than the agreement of a work team leader. Fan Yuanmao, a Communist cadre, has told a story from that time. He had been a district government leader and presided over many meetings for public judgment, that is, meetings to decide how many and who should be executed. At one such meeting, twelve people were to be shot to death. A few more people were called to "escort," or rather to watch, the twelve people being shot. At his order, those to be killed were dragged out into the open field for execution just like pigs were dragged into a slaughterhouse. One of the watchers was mistakenly killed. When asked what to do about that, Fan answered that he would just hand in another form with the name of the mistakenly killed person included, making the total executed thirteen. Easily settled. No other procedure needed. The lives of common people weigh as light as a feather, as a Chinese saying goes.

In some places, father and son, brothers, cousins, were killed together, almost the whole family, just as in the feudal age under the rule of emperors. The process was rather imprecise. The names of those to be executed would be printed in a booklet, which would be given to a cadre of a higher rank for final approval. He would stamp a seal on the page, indicating that the final decision was made. After stamping some pages, the official stood up to get a glass of water. A gust of wind turned two pages over. The man went on stamping till the last page done. The gust of wind saved two people. Years later, the Party admitted that many innocent people were mistakenly executed. They died for nothing. Victims of the overly drastic action of the Party and Mao.

Someone argued that in many dynasties in the history of China (and possibly elsewhere, one might add) lots and lots of innocent people had been mistakenly killed, and so one should not make too big a deal about this. As societies have become more individualistic, we certainly suffer for every needless death, no matter how many or how few are killed. But the Communist Party said at the time that all previous dynasties in history were feudalistic, which is a 'bad' political system; that innocent people were killed under a bad system is fully understandable. But at this time the Chinese Communist Party was boasting that they were implementing socialism, and that the Party always serves the people. Not quite.

In an astonishing example of what can go wrong with "centralized decision making," in February of 1951, Mao called a meeting to decide the rate at which people should be executed. Apparently the rate was set at one per thousand, half of them to be killed first and then a review to confirm the decision based on the situation after the executions began.

Even those Party members who had worked as spies in the former government were deemed traitors and killed; let alone those generals who had betrayed Chiang Kai-shek's government and turned over to the Communist Party; they were also killed. Those generals, if they saw there was no hope of winning, could have gone abroad to live a free, safe life, but apparently they felt their greatest loyalty was to their homeland, regardless of what regime was in power. They were not rewarded for this line of thinking.

Then there was the "Revolt of the Restitution Party," which supposedly involved over 1,300 persons, including 80 Communist Party members. This happened in PuEr Town in Yunnan Province. (PuEr Town is famous for its tea.) Even the Town Party Secretary and the Deputy Director-general of the police were implicated. The First Party Secretary of the Province did not believe the story. Even the district Party organization could not get so many members in such a short time; how could a reactionary organization have achieved it? It turns out the whole story was a fake, cobbled together through coercion and threats, with no evidence at all. One revolutionary sign was posted, drawn up by a primary school teacher under threat. The case was dropped.

As Mr. Wu was the director of the guild, he was appointed by the Party as a representative to the Shanghai people's conference. Then the Korean War broke out at the beginning of the fifties. The Party demanded that all the people in the country should donate money to buy airplanes and guns. Who dared to refuse? They told the people that if the army was not sent into Korea, the United Nations would send troops across Yalu River to invade China. This was nonsense, a total lie. Since Japanese invaders had recently been defeated, who would invade China again? Every wise person can see that as China is such a vast country, no one can conquer and occupy it forever. The Communist Party leaders are apt to use their way of thinking to judge the intension of other people without any evidence to prove that their thinking is right. That's why they always deem innocent people as their enemy or criminals and kill them without gathering any proof or even a second thought.] As the director of the guild, Mr. Wu collected donations from members of the guild besides his own donation. Supported by friends and colleagues, he finished the quota better than that of the other guilds.

Genghua went back to school now, but was a couple of grades behind his former classmates. There were just a few "big students," as they were called, in his new class. But after several months he became ill again and his father decided to take him out of school again.

On the 6th of October, 1950, the Communist army defeated the Tibetan army, which had to surrender. So on the 23rd of May, 1951, the Communist government forced Tibet to sign the Seventeen Point Agreement for the Peaceful Liberation of Tibet. In the agreement, the Communist Party promised autonomy in Tibet, but what they provided was not what the Tibetans considered autonomy. In China proper, they had promised a united government, democracy and freedom of speech, which are still written in their constitution; but when they seized power this turned out to mean one-party rule. And while they finally brought rapid development and relative prosperity to much of the country, it has come at enormous human cost.

How should the leaders maintain a peaceful relationship with minority populations? A wealth of experience and examples have been collected in China's historical record books and legends. Even the feudal rulers, that is, emperors, knew that if they wanted a peaceful relationship with minorities, they had to win their hearts, not just conquer them physically. If they conquered them by force, they would not obey peacefully. The leaders of the Communist Party, especially Mao, who had read a lot of history books, should know the principle. But in reality, those leaders, including Mao himself, are the believers of force and violence. Whenever anything happens, they like to use strong angry words for threatening. They never know lenience. That's why people all over the world often criticize them just in hopes that they can change their attitudes to listen reasonably to others and act to the common standards of the world.

Mr. Wu was not a person strongly interested in fame and political gains. Besides, his health was beginning to decline. Using this as a pretext, he resigned from the position of the representative and the office of the director. As many were competing for such positions, no one opposed his decision. Now he had more free time.

The former maidservant, Ahmei, would come to see the Wu family from time to time, and she brought her little children, eventually four in all. The first three were girls and the last was a son. But then her husband was taken to prison on some pretext like tax-dodging, and he stayed in jail for several years. Ahmei worked in a lane-organized productive group with very low pay. Mrs. Wu often helped Ahmei financially. The grandma also liked her children.

In the outskirts of Wuxi City, at the foot of the famous Plum Hill, on which stood Plum Garden, there was an orphanage. Mr. Wu knew its owner and donated money from time to time. He even asked his friends in Hong Kong for donations. That year, at the beginning of summer, the owner invited Mr. Wu to come and stay in the area for a vacation. The orphanage was a large building with a wide courtyard in the front; the second storey was kept free for donors to come and enjoy the lovely scenery. Wuxi, located \south of the Yangtze River, is itself a scenic city worth visiting. It is connected to Tai Lake, which is much larger than the West Lake in Hangzhou. Nearby is Mount Hui, where famous clay dolls and other art works are made of clay. There is a spring of fresh water there and the taste of the water is especially good. It is full of minerals. Li Garden, on the shore of the Lake, has grottoes in the middle, a long corridor in the eastern part, and a long dam with a six-cornered pavilion in the western part. Standing in the pavilion, one is surrounded by the breathtaking view of the lake and high peaks. The pavilion has twelve wooden columns carved with sixty phoenixes, each group of phoenixes having a dragon in a leading position. In feudal society, the dragon was the embodiment of the emperor and phoenix that of the empress and imperial concubines.

In the orphanage there were two guest rooms on either end of the second floor. In the space in the middle, there was a big statue of Buddha with a few dining tables on each side for guests.

There was a small house a little distance away behind the orphanage, in which lived a family, father, mother and a girl. They had originally been "overseas Chinese," living in Indonesia. The father, Mr. Chen, had been a lawyer there and was suddenly taken ill and could not work anymore. So they had to come to China, as the wife's parents lived in Shanghai. The wife's father was a famous Beijing opera actor, Zhou Xinfang, stage named "Unicorn Boy." He was born in an actor's family and began to perform on the stage at the age of seven. So at first his stage name was "Age-Seven Boy." As the the Chinese characters for "age-seven" are pronounced the same as the characters meaning unicorn, he later changed his stage name to Unicorn Boy.

Her parents supported them and rented the house for them in hopes that their son-in-law would recover in such splendid surroundings. Every day they would go into the Plum Garden through a back door and take a leisurely stroll. The garden was open to tourists. There were many plum trees inside the garden; hence, it was especially lovely and fragrant when the plums were in full bloom.

In the summer of 1951, Mr. Wu and his son took a train to Wuxi City. Since the city had many rivers, water transportation was much utilized. Father and son rode on rickshaws to the nearest riverbank where a boat was available. They were rowed for hours to reach the destination. Since they had left in the morning from Shanghai and arrived in the evening, they went directly to bed after supper.

The next morning, Mr. Chen came to see Mr. Wu. They talked like old friends. At noon, his daughter came to tell him that lunch was ready at home. The girl was a couple of years younger than Genghua. They soon became friends and played together. Father and son often went into the garden to enjoy the scenery. One day they caught a big colorful butterfly and took back to their lodging. The father pressed it between the pages of a book to take back to the city as a specimen.

The weather in summer was often changeable. One afternoon, it poured with rain, with thunder and lightning. It looked as if the sky was leaking. As Genghua was learning to write classical poetry, he suddenly had an inspiration and composed a long poem titled Thunder Storm. His imagination, shaped by local culture, saw the raindrops falling down like pearls on a string, the thunderclaps as the sound of huge drums at the feast of the Jade King in heaven, and the lightning as the light of gigantic candles in the king's banquet room. It was misty outdoors and the contour of the mountains afar became blurred, while the fields nearby flooded with water. When the downpour was over, the sun appeared anew. The sky was especially blue, as if one were looking into the depth of the universe, and a brilliant rainbow hung in the sky. Then the air felt fresh outside and Genghua stood in the courtyard to let the coolness wash over him.

In the city outskirts in summer, people were certainly bothered with mosquitoes. So every bed had a mosquito net hanging over it. Once the neighboring girl caught a dragonfly and put it in the net, saying that dragonflies feed on mosquitoes. So that if any mosquito got into the net, it would be supper for the dragonfly.

Mr. Chen lived there for a long time and knew all the scenic spots. The Chen family took Mr. Wu and Genghua by boat to see the Li Garden. It was constructed in 1927. It has a pathway a thousand meters long, called the Thousand-Pace Corridor. There are also pavilions, arbors and grottoes, beautiful in the way that is typical of garden arrangements in southeastern China. Another renowned spot is Turtle-Head Islet. A big stone, looking like the head of a turtle, stands above the surface of the water. It is surrounded by dramatic scenery. Since 1918, many private gardens also popped up in the vicinity, adding to the ambiance of restful elegance.

Resting for a couple of days, they went to Mount Hui, nation-renowned for clay dolls, which has a productive history of over a thousand years. It developed in Ming Dynasty (1368—1644 AD). The clay near Mount Hui is particularly suitable for this art work. It won't crack when dry or break when bent. Visitors will always buy some when seeing them. Mr. Wu bought a couple for Genghua. There is natural spring water on the mountain, which tastes specially good. Genghua was told about the peculiarity of the spring water. Out of curiosity, he poured this water into a cup and let down some coins one by one into the water. The surface rose a little by a little till 1 mm higher than the brim of the cup without spilling.

Father and son stayed there for a month as there was no more public office affairs that needed his attention. All of a sudden the wife came to tell Mr. Wu that he was wanted for business in Shanghai. They would leave soon. Next day Mr. Wu invited Mr. Chen and his family to have lunch in the city before leaving. So the two families rented a boat for the purpose. The boat moored by the stone steps leading to the back door of a restaurant, where they had steamed fresh water fish. The fish meat was delicious and tender. They also ordered some other dishes. After lunch they went out of the front door of the restaurant and toured the city. Then they came back to the restaurant and went out of the back door and returned by the same boat.

In the evening the manager of the orphanage came upstairs to see Mr. and Mrs. Wu to ask them to adopt a baby. Mrs. Wu did wish to have a girl, as she had only two sons. She followed the manager downstairs to examine all the babies one by one. Most of them were skinny. It was said that the manager embezzled the donated money. One Mrs. Chen, who lived in the house behind the orphanage, said she once witnessed the corpse of a baby being stealthily buried out back. Mrs. Wu saw only one baby that looked well fed. It must have been a new baby. But she had a black birth mark on one cheek, and Mrs. Wu decided not to adopt any baby at all, to the disappointment of the manager.

A few months afterwards, Mr. Chen and his family returned to Shanghai and lived with his father-in-law. The two men became friends and Mr. Chen often visited Mr.•Wu and sometimes stayed for dinner. But the boy and the girl never saw each other again. The adults never thought of bringing the children together to further their friendship.

Now Genghua was fully recovered from TB and went back to school again. And again he met with new faces. In fact he skipped a grade once more and was enrolled directly into the sixth grade.

His brother, the fourth son, was now in the third grade. The school was fifteen minutes walk from home. When Genghua was absent from school, the fourth son was walked to and fro by the auntie staying with them. In every block there was a group of cadres forming so-called Residents Committee to rule over the residents living in this block. Those cadres consisted solely of women, former housewives. They were paid, though not much, by the local government. There was a so-called "Street Committee" to rule over many Residents Committees. There was a police branch to help the Street Committee to maintain law and order in the area. One policeman worked with one Residents Committee. Families living in the same lane formed a small group with a leader, who was a woman either without job or retired. Since the auntie did not work, she helped the cadres with some minor duties. And a couple of years afterwards, she got a job in Suzhou and moved there.

Now Genghua slept on the third floor alone. Every weekday he walked together with his brother to and from the school. He was a few years older than most of his classmates. He could write better compositions than others. He had a good voice and could sing tenor. He even composed a short song and sang in the class. He was a boy of ability, the favorite of the teachers. There was a group of student cadres in every class. One student was appointed the leader and someone would be in charge of student studies and another in charge of student activities, etc. Genghua was the student leader in the class. The whole school had a student committee and he was the student chairman. Only he would soon graduate and enter the middle school for another six years of education.

To enter middle school, every student had to pass an entrance examination. Before graduation every student had to fill out a form with personal information. A woman teacher named Mao was in charge of the class. She advised Genghua to write in the box about his experience as the student committee chairman and the student leader in the class, which might help him to be selected as a student cadre in middle school. But Genghua was too self-confident to think that he would need to be a cadre in middle school, anyway. So he did not write anything in the box. But life did not go on like this, as an inexperienced young boy thought.

Chapter 6 – The First Blow To Capitalists And Genghua Enters Middle School

Even before the Korean War ended, Mao was launching political movements. Chairman Mao loved to set one group against another, like peasants fighting landlords, or like cocks fighting each other to a bloody result. He said, "It is happiness to fight heaven. It is happiness to fight the earth. It is happiness to fight people." But he failed in fighting heaven. He got natural disasters. He also failed in fighting the earth. He got famine. The earth refused to provide enough grain. He was only triumphant in fighting people. How could he fail in fighting common people without weapons, while he controlled the guns? All the political movements he waged were means of fighting people. In fighting his own people, he could enjoy his power and sure victory.

On the 1st of December, 1951, the central committee of the Communist Party passed a decision to carry out the movement which was literally called "Three Anti-'s": anti-corruption, anti-waste, and anti-bureaucratism. This movement targeted at cadres of the government and government-run enterprises; the ones who had power. Mao wanted to limit their power. Right in the wake of this movement, another decision was made to launch another movement, which was literally called "Five Anti-'s": anti theft of state property, anti tax evasion, anti cheating on government contracts, and anti theft of state economic information.

The target of this movement was all the capitalists: everyone who had money or owned property. Mao wanted to deprive them of their wealth. In the feudal society of China, the emperor thought that everything on the land he ruled over was his and everyone on this land had to work for him, like his slaves. Verbally, Mao declared himself as a Marxist–Leninist, but in reality, he was the communist emperor of the Red Dynasty. His actions showed what he thought, though he didn't put it in plain words. Everyone in China was supposed to have only the necessities of life, and no more. If anyone had more than that, Mao would think of a way, or a movement of some kind, to rob them of their wealth. Both movements ended in October, 1952.

On the 26th of January, 1952, the central committee of the Communist Party issued instructions for the Five-Anti-'s movement. In early February, it started in all the big cities, aiming at businessmen. The Party defined them as capitalists. The Party divided Chinese capitalists into two types: bureaucratic capitalists like Chiang Kai-shek, Soong Tse-ven, K'ung Hsiang-hsi, and Chen brothers, were very wealthy and were called the Four Big Capitalist Families by the Communist Party. All the properties they left on the mainland were confiscated. All the others were defined as national (not foreign) capitalists, whose properties had remained theirs for the time being, and who now were the target of the five anti-'s movement. The local governments organized so-called work teams consisting of cadres, workers and shop assistants. Violence was always a part of every movement. Some capitalists were beaten or slapped on their faces. They were forced to make confessions, something they had not had to do so far, in the five categories of anti theft of state property, anti tax evasion, anti cheating on government contracts, and anti theft of state economic information. It was called face-to-face fighting. Quite a few capitalists committed suicide.

Statistics showed that during these two movements, in the whole country, 184,270 persons were arrested, 119,355 party members expelled from the party, and 133,760 died or disabled, including those making suicide or beaten to death, and tortured to die in jails and labor reform camps.

Mr. Cheng in Suzhou, a friend of Mr. Wu's, killed himself under the pressure he could no longer bear. He had a son who was then working in Hong Kong by name of Cheng Zongchuan. He had been engaged to the daughter of Mr. Shen in Shanghai. Once Mr. Shen went to Hong Kong on business and the young Cheng received him. Cheng had made every possible comfortable arrangement for him and he liked the young man very much. So when he was back to Shanghai he asked Mr. Wu to be the matchmaker because Mr. Wu knew the young man's father. After the suicide of his father and when he lost job in Hong Kong, the young man came back to Shanghai intending to marry the daughter of Mr. Shen, but Mr. Shen, seeing that the young man had no father and no job, refused to marry his daughter to him. He could not go back to Hong Kong to look for another job and had to ask the local government for a job and got married to some other woman later. He settled in Shanghai. Under the rule of the Party, people had nowhere to apply for any job. The communist government allotted jobs to people as government cadres thought fit. Those who wanted to have a better job had to bribe cadres.

Therefore, the young man hated Mr. Shen. Later in the Cultural Revolution he organized a so-called rebellious group and went to the house of Mr. Shen. He made the old man kneel on the ground and slapped his face hard as the revenge for turning down his request to marry his daughter, as originally agreed upon.

After the suicide of several capitalists, the government changed its strategy. The work teams performed back-to-back fights so that no violence could happen anymore. The face-to-face fight was like this: the employees were told to gather in a big room with the capitalist, in other words the business owner, their employer, standing at one end of the room, facing his employees. Then the employees revealed all the crimes of their employer in the five categories, some pointing their fingers in his face. Some angry employees would beat the employer or insult him in public. The back-to-back fight was like this: the employees were not allowed to see their employers. They just revealed to the work team members crimes their employers supposedly had committed. So the workers did not beat or abuse the employer directly.

As Mr. Wu had always been considerate and polite to his workers, no one really attacked him. Besides, he was a careful man and had done nothing wrong in the five categories; although his partners may have been less prudent. The actual goal of this movement, as every capitalist knew, but could not say, was that the communist government wanted to squeeze money out of their pockets. Every capitalist had to pay a fine, some more and some less, for their guilt in the five categories. Mr. Wu had to sell the refrigerator, a set of sofas, and some jewelry for cash, which he handed in for the charge of tax-dodging. Of course, his partners gave money to the government, too. No one could get round it without paying the fine lawfully inflicted on them. It was secretly called among capitalists as the first financial blow on the national capitalists. The second blow would soon come in a name very pleasing to the ear.

When the capitalists got the blow financially, there were still people who had money. Those were doctors who had their own offices to receive patients. They raked in a lot of money every day. When the capitalists sold things to raise money, they bought those things at low prices. One day Mr. Wu went to see his doctor Yue Wenzhao, he saw the set of sofas he had sold were in the waiting room. But that was okay for him. When he went home and told it to his wife, the family got a good laugh. Things are supposed to be in circulation in the human world. No one can hold anything for ever, and ever. Even dynasties will change hands. So will the Chinese communist regime. Some day.

After summer vacation in 1954, Genghua attended Xiangming Middle School, just a block from the primary school, where his little brother was now in the fourth grade. He would walk his brother to his school first and then go on to middle school himself. Middle school in China was divided into two levels: junior middle school and senior middle school, three years for each.

Throughout the schooling process, and especially in universities, the birth status of a student was very important for his future. The first category consisted of those born into the family of a party cadre, second in a worker family or family of shop assistants, then a family of intellectuals like teachers and doctors, down to capitalist families, and the worst category included landowners and reactionaries. But there was always an exception. If someone from a capitalist family could flatter the Party leader, he would be put in an important position at work. Mao had said that a person could not choose his birth status, but could choose what road in life he wanted to follow. When someone flattered a Party leader, it was deemed that he was loyal to the Party and was following the socialist road the Party pointed out for him. He was considered to have betrayed his own family. Funny theory. So far so good.

The class Genghua was in had two more so-called big students besides himself. The teacher appointed student cadres by their family background. Therefore, although Genghua was talented, the teacher did not give him any special position since he came from capitalist family and never said anything to ingratiate himself with the teacher. But a girl student from the same kind of family was put in charge of class activities as she could sweet-talk the teacher. Later, Genghua came to understand that flattery to the teacher was valued more than talent; but it was not his cup of tea.

Genghua commenced to read books of materialist dialectics and books by Marx, Lenin, Stalin and Mao. At first Genghua felt what they wrote sounded reasonable, especially Mao's books about theory of united government, democracy and freedom of speech for people. Later, nevertheless, he found that Mao's actions did not resemble his written prescriptions. Genghua could still remember clearly what the politics teacher had said in his class: that everyone had to speak positively, had to say that he loved the Party, that he wanted to follow the Party forever; but in reality, he could act otherwise, because according to the party's own theory, a person's thinking would only evolve from a backward status to an advanced status through a slow process. That is to say that a person had to have a changing process in his mind from not loving the Party to deeply loving the Party. From this teaching, Genghua understood that a person could be two-faced. He might declared that he was a good man, in public, and he might embezzle money on the side. And it seems that many communist cadres did just that, including Mao.

There were two kinds of political organizations among students. Students in primary and junior middle schools could join Young Pioneers, every member wearing a red tie. Students in senior middle schools and universities or over eighteen could join Youth League. They were deemed the successor of the Party. As members of Young Pioneers were too young to work independently, a Youth League member in senior middle school was assigned to be the guide of Young Pioneers, one guide for Young Pioneer members in one class.

The guide in the class Genghua was in was an arrogant girl. As he was not a member of the Young Pioneers, he saw no reason to show esteem to her. He did not know at that time that all this would bring him obstacle on his road of life. Thus he made a bad impression on the teacher in charge of his class, too. But many classmates were nice to him because he was a good student, always had good marks in tests, and liked to help others with their studies. All in all, he had a bad start in middle school. Every school had politics classes to teach students the communist ideas of politics. In politics class, teachers would emphasize two things. One is that the final goal of the Communist Party is to liberate all peoples in the world, as they are living in "deep water and hot fire" under the capitalist system. In other words, they must conquer the whole world and put it under their reign of proletarian dictatorship. The other is that political power comes from the barrel of a gun. In other words, they must strengthen their armed forces so that they can complete their first goal to rule the whole world. They believe in conquering others by force only, and never thought of how to win the hearts of people for everlasting harmony and peace.

His life in the first grade in junior middle school was just so-so. Bad luck for him was yet to come. After school, he went to pick his brother in the primary school and they walked home together. Once when he went to the primary school, the teacher Mao, who had been the teacher in charge of his sixth grade class, wanted him to give a message to his father, Mr. Wu. The teacher was a woman, who had a brother. The brother wanted to marry and had nowhere to live, because all the housing was controlled by the government. Anyone in need of housing had to apply for it to the housing department. The procedures were complicated and took a long time. The brother could not wait for a long time to get married. The woman teacher knew that no one lived in the ground floor room of Mr. Wu's house and asked to sublet it to her brother. Mr. Wu agreed and signed a contract with the brother, stating that he could not use the full bathroom upstairs. He could use the half bathroom downstairs. At that time the old woman working for the Wu family had gone back to Ningpo. The family hired another younger woman for the housework and she slept in grandma's room. Soon the newly-wedded couple moved in.

Genghua's health had improved by the time he was sixteen, just as the fortune-teller had predicted. As he was now at the age to join the Youth League, a League member in his class talked to him and suggested that he should apply for the membership, but he rejected. He had no faith in it and did not want that kind of obligation. A Youth League member could easily become a Party member and acquire various privileges, but many people are not cut out for politics.

In the middle school, every class had a class meeting, at which no lessons were given. There were only discussions about class affairs or some criticisms of some students for their faults. The teacher in charge of the class presided over it. Some students reported that they had lost something like a pen, or even pocket money they left in their satchels. So the teacher warned everyone to take care of personal things. One student suspected a girl sitting in the first row did the theft, but no proof. The student wanted to test it. One day he dropped a one-yuan note on the floor just beside the suspected girl, and asked, "Did anyone drop some money?" The girl looked at it and said that it was hers. She picked up the banknote and put into her own pocket. But it could not be proven that she was the one stealing things. So the student was laughed at for his stupid test. Then another student accidentally caught the girl red-handed. So the girl had to return the things she had stolen and made a self-criticism at one of the class meetings, sobbing.

In another class meeting, a student criticized the teacher. A boy in the class had been summoned to the army. A girl student had gone to Australia, for her parents lived there. The teacher often said in class that he had missed the girl student, but never referred to the boy student. The student criticizing the teacher said that the teacher should refer to the boy student more frequently as he went to serve the country, while the girl student was a traitor, not worth remembering. At that time, anyone going abroad was deemed or even mentioned as a traitor. Everyone should stay in China to show that he loved the Party, even if he was persecuted by the government. Another weird theory was that committing suicide was deemed to be betrayal to the Party. He was supposed to endure any persecution or even torment by the Party to show his loyalty.

When he was in the equivalent of eighth grade, he had a new classmate named Bai Yinglin, who was transferred here. His father had grown up in northeast China, then gone to Germany for university education and married a Jewish girl there. When the Nazis began to kill Jews, Bai's father protected his mother since China and Germany were not at war. His parents came to Shanghai during the Second World War. His father worked as an engineer in some research institute and his mother taught German language in Shanghai Foreign Languages Institute. They lived in an apartment house on the fourth floor. The house was owned by an Arabic man, who later sold the house to the government and went back to Arabia. The rent was very high because they had heating and hot water in winter. Most houses in Shanghai have no such equipment. People living in such houses use two thick quilts in cold weather. Some even keep shirt and pullover on when lying in bed. Most well-to-do families in Shanghai put hot water bottles between quilts at night to keep warm, especially for old people. What was the standard for a well-to-do family at that time was that the family should have a bank account with a balance of a couple of hundred yuan. If anyone had ten thousand yuan in bank, he was deemed rich.

Genghua got familiar with the boy, Bai. When Genghua walked home, he would pass by the apartment house of the boy. So they both left school at the same time and walked home together. Oftentimes the boy would invite him to go into his suite. They did homework together. Most of the time the boy's mother was at home, because if there were no classes, she did not need to go to her college. Genghua had learned some English before 1949. He could talk a little with the mother. After communist government came, they forbade English teaching in primary schools and junior middle schools. It was only taught in some senior middle schools and universities. But Russian was taught in most schools and universities. People sang Russian songs and read Russian novels, both translated into Chinese. China called Russia the big old brother. Anyone who dared to criticize Russia, the Soviet Union, was deemed to criticize China. Woe to him.

Genghua's classmate Bai spoke German at home and was learning English from some Englishman. So he knew three languages. It is an advantage for some child whose parents got international marriage and could speak different languages.

Sometimes when there was a lot of homework, they could not finish in a few hours. So they had dinner together at Bai's home. After dinner, they continued doing homework till ten at night. As Genghua went home, Bai would see him downstairs to the street. Often on the street they would see a pedlar shouldering a thick stick with two wooden boxes on either end. There was a small oven inside one box and a pot on the oven. The other box contained bowls, chopsticks, spoons, and noodles and wantons. The boys would often order a bowl each with noodle and wanton mixed together. They would stand by the boxes and held the bowl in one hand and chopsticks in the other. When finishing, Genghua would pay the pedlar and went home alone. Bai would return upstairs. This was their enjoyable recollection in their later years.

They had another classmate by the surname of Yang, whose father was a professor in the Shanghai Conservatory of Music and a famous conductor. When there was little homework, Yang would invite Bai and Genghua to his home. Yang family had a pianoforte and Bai liked to play on the keyboard some music of his own impromptu creation on the spot to the laughter of Yang's little sister.

Bai knew a neighbor, a boy of his age, by the surname of Liu, who lived in the suite on the floor under his. Sometimes they gathered in Bai's suite to play a few rounds of card game. Once they went to Liu's suite and Liu's father taught them how to play bridge. It was the first time Genghua learned to play bridge. Liu was a student cadre in his class. He was not in the same school with Bai and Genghua.

In 1954, the second son of Mr. Wu graduated from a two-year course in Jiaoda University and was assigned work in Shanghai Diesel Engine Factory. He still lived with his own mother.

Since the Wu family did not have a living room any more, if
guests came, they just sat in the bedroom on the second floor. Now
this room served as bedroom, sitting room, and dining room as well.
The third and fourth sons slept on the third floor. Once on a weekend Genghua invited Bai home to have dinner. Bai came early in the
afternoon and the parents, Genghua and Bai played mahjong. Bai
loved to learn how to play it. At dinner, they had Chinese dishes. At
home, Bai always had western food his mother cooked. So it was a
change of taste for him. After dinner they continued to play till late
at night. Bai went home.

Bai could play the mouth organ, so he joined the mouth organ
band in that school and Bai joined it. Genghua joined the student
choir and sang tenor. Once a week they would go to their respective
groups to practice. During every major festival, the school would
organize performances for the students in the school auditorium.
There were singing, dancing, drama, mouth organ, etc. Once there
was a performance of gymnastics, with a set of uneven bars on the
stage. A girl performed her dazzling routine, her coach standing

by as a spotter. When she swung her foot upwards, her bare sole hit the face of the coach, who was standing too close. The coach seemed not to be hurt, as he was so strong, with thick face muscles. Students in the audience began joking that one typically slaps with the hand, but this girl used her foot. Young people's insensitivity; but as far as we ever knew, he was not in fact hurt.

Li DingGuo was a member of the mouth organ group, but he was a student belonging to the senior middle school. He was a nice guy and became a friend of Bai and Genghua. Once in a while on Sundays, they would go out together to a movie or some restaurant for refreshments. Soon Li graduated from the middle school and was enrolled in Shanghai Second Medical Institute to be a doctor. Then they seldom met. But Genghua learned in the so-called Cultural Revolution that Li killed himself by injecting air into his vein. Many talented people in China died this way or by other means during this movement and others. Incredibly, some people who had been living abroad, returned to China to show their love for the Communist Party; and died in the political movements, because they were looked upon as spies from abroad. At the time, it was felt that such tragedies would never happen in "democratic" countries.

Generally, on spring vacation the teacher in charge of a class would take his students, on a volunteer basis, somewhere like a park. They would play some group game like handkerchief throwing. Students crouched on the ground in a circle, face inward. One student with a handkerchief ran round the circle. He or she would throw down the handkerchief behind the back of a student without the notice of the student and kept running. On the next round when he or she got to that student, if the student did not find the handkerchief behind him or her, the student running would slap on his or her back, meaning he or she was the loser, who would get up and ran with the handkerchief. The student who caught him or her would take his or her place. Other times, they would rent a few boats and row them on the artificial lake. Genghua wrote a long poem and translated it in later years:

> The setting sun reflects on the golden waves;
> The ripples follow in the wake of the light boat.

> *Peach trees intervene among the willows at the lakeside,*
> *On the center of the lake float a pair of wild geese.*

Once the teacher took the students on a visit to a public grave-yard, where soldiers were buried who had died in the war when attacking Shanghai. The teacher asked Genghua to write an elegiac speech and read it before the tombs of these soldiers as a salute. They went there on a Saturday and accordingly Genghua recited the speech with feeling. Many years later, when Genghua thought of it, he felt ridiculous, because those soldiers had died as cannon fodder—not for the Chinese people, but to fulfill the ambitions of the national leadership, who tread on the bodies of innocent men and women.

One day in his home, Bai told Genghua that his parents had de-cided to move back to Germany. They sensed that the situation was worsening in China, even if it was not yet clear what was going to happen. He told Genghua what his first name Yinlin meant. Yin in Chinese meant to answer (the call), and Lin meant Berlin. He should answer any call to go to Berlin to serve his mother's moth-erland. And after he left with his parents, some school authorities, teachers, and classmates called him a traitor and other names. But a person of dual nationality has the right to choose. If he betrayed anything, on his father's side, it was a tyrannical regime that had promised people freedom while betraying their trust.

Some ancient Chinese scholars maintained the notion that the people were the foundation of the country. The Communist Party teaches Chinese people that they should love the country; but they mean that the people should love the Party, especially the Party leaders, not the people as nation. They limit the meaning of "love your country" so that anyone who criticizes the leaders is consid-ered not to love the country. Like the saying in 1960s America, "Love It or Leave It." No room for discussion. No freedom of speech. No democratic airing of legitimate differences of view.

Before Bai left China, he asked Genghua to write down his ad-dress in his notebook so that he could write to Genghua when he got to Germany. Genghua could not refuse. He was only afraid that correspondence with anyone abroad might cause him trouble because it was the open secret that letters from abroad would be opened for examination by government personnel.

Having passed the entrance examination to the senior middle school, Bai and Genghua were accepted into the first grade of the senior middle school, equivalent to tenth grade. Bai attended the class only for one day. He left the next day. It was at the beginning of September. After several month, Genghua received a letter from his former classmate. From then on, they kept regular correspondence. Only Genghua was very careful about what he should not write in reply. Bai had correspondence with Liu, too. But a few months later, Bai wrote to Genghua that Liu dropped the correspondence for fear of getting into trouble by writing to a traitor.

In 1956, a financial movement began which was called the socialist reform of national capitalists. The goal was to take over the factories, stores, and rental houses belonging to Chinese business owners (capitalists) and put them under the full control of the communist government. It was called merging, but it looked like confiscation. And every capitalist had to apply to the government to be merged, in other words offer to hand over his own property to the government, just like a lone pedestrian in the street has to give his money to a robber. Who would dare to refuse? Even more ridiculous, the government had to approve the application. What if the government did not approve it? Well, that would never happen. When a robber takes your money, does he stop in mid-act and wait for the pedestrian to beg him to accept. Don't laugh. Things like this did happen. Applications were approved, and the business owners paraded over to the local government house to show their happiness and to celebrate the successful merging.

By way of compensation, the government gave the national capitalists five percent of the value of their properties every year. The value was determined by the government. The payment was called Fixed Interests. But the fixed interests were first established only for seven years, with the question of renewing the terms to be determined at the end of the seven years by the Party. This great political task was victoriously finished in due time. The only lucky break for the capitalists was that they were allowed to keep their personal valuables for the time being (but not for long). The Party kept looking into the pockets of the people and taking anything of value. Luckily, during this movement, we did not hear about any suicides.

After the government took over all the properties, a capitalist was given a position in his former factory or store to get a little pay in addition to the fixed interests he was receiving. If he was the owner of rental houses, he would work in the housing department of the local government. Only he could not make any decision without the consent of the Party secretary, if he was still in a leading position. He was just a decoration there to show how lenient the Party was. A story went about the Donglaishun Restaurant in Beijing. After merging, its name was changed to Nation Restaurant. It still sold lamb, or rather mutton, but the meat was not so delicious as before since it was run by a Party hack who had no knowledge and experience of the business. So customers said that the capitalist mutton had lost its savory taste after the socialist reform.

As for those capitalists who were old or in poor health, they were just retired and lived solely on the Fixed Interests. This was the case with Mr. Wu. Every aspect of his life was affected. Since the beginning of the fifties, playing mahjong was forbidden. If Mr. Wu wanted to chant some Buddhist sutras, he could only do it in secret, of course. Any superstitious action was criticized, and later forbidden, too. No worshiping of gods, no fortune-telling, no reference to the occult. Of course, rumors went around that some of the Party leaders or high-ranking government officials still sent for a famous fortune-teller and still followed their own superstitious beliefs.

Extramarital sex was also banned. Offenders were not sent to jail but to labor reform camp, which was far worse. In prison, at least the sentence was a set number of years; but not labor reform. The period, long or short, depended on the whim of the camp's Party leaders. However, it was an open secret that this ban did not apply to the very top. Mao is blamed for forcing himself on many women and in some cases causing their later suicide or execution.

The government organized those retired capitalists to meet once every month to study what the Party wanted them to study. It was called Deity Meeting, suggesting that they live in retirement, happy as a deity (though no one can tell if a deity is happy or not). Mr. Wu often asked for leave from the meeting on the pretense of feeling not well. But no one really cared. Even the government cadre in charge of it did not care. It was just one more formality to go through.

The retired capitalists, though they had plenty of free time, could not play mahjong any more. That was considered a sign of a so-called capitalist life style and was strictly forbidden. Some of them just played cards by themselves; solitaire. And they were also allowed to visit each other. But the cadres of the Resident Committee were government spies and would report anything they thought suspicious to the police branch.

In any election year, people who were employed voted where they worked and people without work would vote in the office of Resident Committee. If the government wanted, say, three people as the so-called people's representatives, they would choose three persons they favored and put their names on a list. The voters just went to make marks under the names. So voting was easy. If any voters dared to vote for less than the three selected options, or refused to vote, he would be deemed not loyal to the Party. Then ill fortune would befall him. If any voters were sick in bed, the cadres would take a voting box to him or her; the votes had to be one hundred percent to show that all the people supported the government, the Party.

Once a young worker in a factory, in order to make a good impression on a leading cadre, crossed out a name on the list, and put the name of the leading cadre on it, and voted for him. Even for that he got criticized. What if he had thought of writing in the name of a fellow worker, someone whom the factory Party secretary did not like? One misstep may cause everlasting regret.

CHAPTER 8 – THE ANTI-RIGHTIST MOVEMENT AND ANOTHER
CLOSE CALL

On the 20th of April, 1956, Mao gave a speech about "Double-Hundred Policy," the meaning of which was "To let hundred flowers bloom, to let hundred (different) opinions expressed." Then the minister of the Central Party Propaganda Ministry, Lu Dingyi, made a speech to explain it to all the intellectuals that they had to have independent thinking, they would have freedom of debate, freedom of creativeness and criticizing, freedom of expressing, insisting on, and reserving their own opinions. It was so sweet to hear, but only fools believed it and gave out their opinions boldly.

On the 1st of May, 1957, the People's Daily published the document "Instructions about Rectification Movement," which was passed at the Central Committee of Communist Party on the 27th of April. The Party decided to have the rectification movement within the Party for anti-bureaucratism, anti-sectarianism, and anti-subjectivism. The Party called upon people outside the Party, upon people the country over, to express their opinions, to criticize the Party and government, and to help the Party in their rectification movement. The request sounded earnest. This was the sole movement that aimed at the Party itself. But wait and see what would be the result.

Many people in the country, especially the intellectuals, capitalists, and others who were less likely to benefit from communism and who were foolish enough to take the bait, did criticize the Party for its many obvious wrongdoings. Even the newspapers followed suit. At that time, people really thought that the Party was open to sincere criticism as it had said. It was a snare that many naive people fell in. Then the "anti-rightist" movement began. The so-called general rightist opinions included these: complaints of peasants that their life was worse than before and that the life of workers in the cities was better than that of peasants — the policy requiring peasants to sell a high quota of the harvest to the government forced the peasants themselves to starve. Others were to cancel the political lessons in schools and universities; to have the freedom of moving to other cities or from the countryside to the city; to have the freedom of speech and publication; to criticize the wrong-doings in the previous movements; to criticize Chinese interference in the Korean War when the money used in the war could have been used for the improvement of the life of their own people or in the construction of China; to criticize the Soviet Union for their soldiers raping Chinese women in 1946 when they occupied the northeast of China after driving the Japanese army away; to criticize one-party tyranny; to demand equal opportunity in government elections (because there were some so-called democratic parties in China); etc.

However, on the 8th of June, the People's Daily had an editorial "Why Is This?" on the first page. It mentioned the term "Rightists." On the 12th of June, Mao wrote an article, "Things Are Changing" and circulated it within the Party. On the 14th, the People's Daily published another editorial, "The Bourgeoisie Direction of the Wenhui Daily." It was said that this editorial was written by Mao. It blamed the Wenhui Daily and the Brightness Daily, two newspapers managed by Party members, for their criticisms of the Party. Then the anti-rightist movement began.

It was said that Mao had said that the rectification movement was just a strategy to "lure snakes out of their holes." Who were

the snakes? It seemed to be the rightists Mao meant. Mao estimated that about five percent of the population in China were
rightists. This was really subjectivism of Mao doing so, as he gave
a fixed number for the rightists without counting yet, even when
the movement just began. The number should be counted when the
result came out from the reality. Not before. On the fifteenth of October, the Central Committee of the Party issued another document
"Standards to Decide on Rightists." There were six rules for deter-
mining who were rightists:

1. Anti socialist system, such as opposing the basic economic
policies of the Party and government; negating the achievements
of socialist revolution and construction; insisting on capitalist
standpoint.

2. Opposing proletarian dictatorship and democratic central-
ism, such as attacking the fight for anti-imperialism; negating the
foreign policy of the government; negating five movements: attacking executions of reactionaries, opposing the reform of capitalists
and capitalist intellectuals, demanding to replace the laws and cultural education of socialism with those of capitalism.

3. Opposing the leadership of the Communist Party in political life, such as opposing the leadership of the Communist Party in
economy and culture, attacking the leading organizations and leaders of the Communist Party and the government for the purpose
of opposing socialism and the Party, slandering the revolutionary
activities of the Party.

4. Disrupting the unity of people for the purpose of opposing
socialism and the Party, such as instigating people against the Party
and the government; instigating the disruption between workers
and peasants; instigating the disruption among minorities; slandering the socialist camp; instigating the disruption among peoples of
different countries in socialist camp.

5. Actively organizing and joining cliques against socialism and
the party, such as plotting to overthrow the leadership of the Party
anywhere; instigating riot against the Party and government.

6. Anyone who gives advice, introducing someone, giving information, or reporting secrets of revolutionary organizations, to those who committed the above crimes.

Four rules for identifying extreme rightists:

1. The ambitious persons, the leaders, and the chief plotters in the rightist activities.

2. Those giving opinions of guiding principles, and actively advocating such opinions.

3. Those who are especially firm and abominable in the activities against socialism and the Party.

4. Those who always act against people in history, and actively joining in the reactionary activities in this anti-rightists movement.

There were 552,877 rightists in China. The whole population in China in 1957 was 642,380,000 people. The important rightists included Zhang Bojun, head of the Brightness Daily newspaper, Chu Anping, chief editor of that newspaper, Luo Longji, head of the Wenhui Daily newspaper, and Pu Xixiu, chief editor of that newspaper. One of the rightists among capitalists was Wang Kangnian, whose opinion was that if the government bought the properties from the capitalists, as they declared, they had to pay twenty years of fixed interests, not only seven years, as the rate was five percent. His calculation was absolutely correct. Actually, what the rightists had said were all proved correct by the facts happened. As for the fixed interests, at the end of the seven years, the Party decided to continue paying it for another three years. Ten years altogether. Then the Cultural Revolution began and no one mentioned it any more. So now, there are still ten years of the fixed interests remaining to be paid to the Chinese national capitalists, or their sons, or their grandsons, or their great grandsons. If it is not paid off for the remaining ten years, the Party always owes the repayment. If the Party does not pay off the debt, they will always be a debtor, a matter to lose face. A shame.

Mr. Wu was sick at home. So he didn't say anything in public. He was, of course, not a rightist. One of his friends, Mr. Gan, was arrested and died in the prison, known later from his family.

What opinion he had given for the arrest was not known even to his family. The Party could arrest anyone for whatever excuses they thought fit. Whatever they thought unfit to their ideas or benefits was the reason to put anyone under their custody. No human rights in their eyes.

Then what became of the rightists? Some lost positions and were forced to clean bathrooms. Their salaries were duly reduced to the level of a cleaner's. Some were sent to the labor reform camps. The labor was so heavy, plus a great famine took place later, many died of hunger or disease. All got unjust punishment.

All the rightists had a "rightist cap" as it was called even in the newspaper. It was actually an invisible cap, only recorded in their personal files. As the files followed them everywhere they went like having a cap always on head. Hence, the name. Since 1985, some rightists were restored to their citizenship, but they were still called "uncapped rightists," which meant that though their caps were removed, they were still deemed different from other people.

During so-called Cultural Revolution, those people, no matter whether still capped or uncapped, were criticized or even beaten. In 1977, all the wrong cases were redressed, including rightist cases, almost twenty years after the anti-rightist movement. Until May of 1980, most of the rightist cases were rehabilitated. Now 533,222 out of 552,877 rightists were no longer rightists, no longer called "uncapped rightists." That meant that 97% of the rightist cases had been wrongly adjudicated. In 1978, after twenty years, out of 552,877, only a little more than 100,000 rightists survived. It meant how many wrong cases were in this movement and how many victims died.

On November 13, 2005, Shi Ruping, a retired professor from Shandong University, together with some other professors and their families, signed an open letter to National People's Congress and the State Council demanding that the Party should make self-criticism and apologies to the intellectual victims for their political persecution, and make reasonable and enough compensations. In three months, they got 1,500 supporters.

In 2007, it was the fiftieth anniversary of the anti-rightist movement. Sixty-one survivors in Beijing signed an open letter demanding that the Party should openly declare the rehabilitation of the whole anti-rightist movement, not just for the individual rightists. But the Party persisted in their wrong-doings and refused to make the rehabilitation.

Through this movement, Mao and the Party intended to quench all the opposing voices or even to control people's thoughts. Anyone who dared to say anything different from what the Party wanted them to say would get punishment. It was said that Mao liked to read history books and learn strategies from those used by ancient strategists in all the historical events, stratagems for how to seize power, how to defeat his political enemies, how to make false moves in the war, how to cheat by sweet talk, and how to win the hearts of people by promising them all sorts of benefits so that people could support him in his goal to gain power—promises he would never have to keep.

There is a principle in the "Art of War" which states that if the number of your forces is double that of the enemy, you can attack; if the number of your forces is ten times of that of your enemy, you can surround them. Mao learned this principle and put it in his own words: it's better to sever one finger than to injure ten. It means that in every battle, you would better wipe out all the enemy's army rather than simply defeat them. So Mao's tactic was to annihilate Chiang Kai-shek's army, one division at a time, till Chiang Kai-shek's forces grow weaker and his own grow stronger. He succeeded and finally drove Chiang to Taiwan. Although Chiang Kai-shek was said to have been trained in a Japanese military academy, no one ever said anything about him having studied Chinese history for war strategies. The only book he is known to have read was the collection of family letters of Zeng Guofan, a commander and courtier in Qing Dynasty, who had organized an army of his own to conquer the rebellious army of the Peaceful Kingdom between 1851 and 1864. But Chiang Kai-shek learned from this book only how to improve personal morals. A sure loser in his political career.

Like certain emperors in the former dynasties, Mao never listened to different opinions. He thought that he was always right. So that was why he wanted to start the anti-rightist movement: to teach people a lesson—to shut up. Now, King You of the West Zhou Dynasty (1121–771 BC), wielding his tyrant's power all over the kingdom, promulgated a law making it a crime to criticize him in one's mind alone. But who could know what thought was in which one's mind? At least those persecuted in the anti-rightist movement were people who had said or written something that sounded like criticism of the Party.

Classical Chinese writings include more than stratagems for winning war; they include the wisdom garnered over centuries guiding rulers in winning the loyalty of the people and to rule the country well. Mao never learned those lessons. Mao disturbed people's life from the beginning of his reign to the end, by staging continuous upheavals.

Mao was not the only one responsible for the self-inflicted disasters in China. He had many accomplices who supported him in all his ideas. Few dared disagree with Mao. Premier Zhou always agreed to whatever Mao said. Deng Xiaoping, the so-called general designer of the post-Mao open policy, never opposed Mao when Mao was alive. Only when Mao was dead, he changed all Mao's policies about China's economical development. When he came into power, he took a shar[turn off the socialist road and generally followed a capitalist course, financially. This benefited some of the Chinese people, creating a prosperous veneer, especially in towns and cities. It seems that the only comrade who dared to say no to Mao was Peng Dehuai, former minister of the defense ministry. In a letter to Mao, he criticized Mao's mistakes and said what the Chinese people wanted to say. Of course, he was removed from office immediately and died tragically in the Cultural Revolution.

It is very important to use the right strategies in wars, especially so when the forces are almost equal on both fighting sides. If the forces on the two fighting sides are not equal, it is a different thing. The strong forces will certainly conquer the weak forces. The main strategy Mao and the Communist Party used was to gather enough soldiers, using their bodies, their lives, to attack the enemy, since Mao did not have better weapons. If they could sacrifice the lives of ten soldiers to kill one enemy soldier, they would do it without hesitation. They never counted the lives expended in order to achieve their aims.

On the contrary, Chiang Kai-shek and his generals only knew to use better weapons, but those were not always dependable in the wars of that time. When their army was surrounded by that of the Communist Party and could not break through the defensive line even using their more sophisticated weapons, they just surrendered. They wanted to save the lives of their soldiers. If they could have used the bodies of their soldiers in addition to their armaments to form a strong detachment, like a sharp knife, they could have broken through the enemy line at a certain point. But that would have required the willingness to sacrifice the lives of soldiers.

The anti-rightist movement affected even young people in school. The school authorities called upon faculties and students to give their opinions and criticize the Party. They wrote their opinions on so-called Big-Character-Posters and put up the papers on walls or hung it on lines in the corridors and classrooms. Genghua wrote one opinion about Chinese history lessons. He thought it was a waste to learn Chinese history three times, once in primary schools, then in junior middle schools again, and in senior middle schools once more. For this, he was criticized in a student meeting in the school auditorium together with a few other students, who might have also given improper opinions. They mentioned his correspondence with Bai, whom they thought of as a traitor. Genghua had to take all his personal letters from Bai to the school and declare that he would stop the correspondence. But the teachers could not make up their minds on this, as it was a matter of international relations and protecting China's public image. They just returned the letters to Genghua and said nothing more. So Genghua kept in touch with Bai and said nothing of it to him in his letters of reply. Luckily, the Party decided that there were no rightists among middle school students as they were still too young to have independent thinking. But the faculty were not so lucky. Quite a few of them were found to be rightists. A teacher of English was sent to clean the bathrooms. He knew three foreign languages. Students quickly drew the conclusion that any teacher who no longer appeared in class must have been designated a rightist. Some of the older teachers died before their cases were redressed.

Students in universities were also not lucky, and many were labeled rightists. A next door neighbor of Genghua, a young man named Chen, was capped as a rightist as he was a student in a university in Beijing. Genghua was spared this fate due to his poor health that had kept him home for many years, so that he was still in middle school at an age when he should have been in university.

Sometimes Genghua recalled the friendship with the neighbor Chen, a year older than he. He came to know Chen as soon as the Wu family moved into the new house. There were some other young people in the same lane. They formed a drama group and often rehearsed a drama written all by themselves. On the night of the National Day in 1951, a stage was put up at one end of the lane and some performances were shown on it. They acted their drama to the applause of the residents.

There was no more spring vacation for merry-making in the school. The school authorities used the period instead to drive the students to the countryside or somewhere else as free labor force. Genghua's class was sent to a construction site. What they did was to carry the bricks from where they were stored to where workers were working. The students got in a line. The first one lifted five bricks and gave to the next student and then the next one till the last one, who put down the bricks in piles so that the workers could lay their hands on easily. When some students were assigned with some other tasks and the number carrying bricks was reduced, someone thought of a way to solve the problem. Each student expanded the distance several meters away from the next student. The first one lifted up only two bricks and threw them to the next student, who caught the bricks in the air. Then he passed the bricks to still the next one in the same way. The last student, when catching them, put on piles. Genghua joked that after such practice, they could pass things easily from a distance when back at school. It was also good training for basketball players.

On the construction site, the boys slept in a big long shelter built of bamboo. In the tent there were two rows of long bamboo beds, one row above the other. The boys lay down on the long bamboo beds one by one, with all heads at one end and all feet at the other end, like sardines arranged in a can. Genghua slept on the upper row. When he climbed up, the bamboo creaked. Every time someone moved, it creaked. The girl students slept in a big room on some mats. They had hot water and a tub for bathing. But the boys had to wash themselves in cold tap water in the open air.

At the end of every semester, even P. E. Class had the final test to give students marks. The testing items were horizontal bar, parallel bars, vaulting horse, long jump, high jump, 100 meters run and 1,500 meters run, for male students. The performance on the first three items was simple. The items for the female students were uneven bars, balance beam, also long jump and high jump, 60 meters run, and 800 meters run. The student cadres had guaranteed to the teacher in charge of the class that everyone in the class should pass all the items, but one male student was short and thin. In the 1,500 meters run, he ran and ran, but his speed got slower and slower. If he kept like this, he would certainly fail in this item. So two big students, lifting him up by the arms, carried him to the finish line, just in time for the C mark.

Chapter 9 – The Great Leap-Forward & Steel-Making Movement

Barely had the anti-rightist movement victoriously completed, in November, 1957, when Mao put up another idea. China should overtake Great Britain in fifteen years in the output of iron and steel and major products. By then the total goal of iron and steel production should be 10,700,000 tons. It was passed as an official decision of the Party on the 17th of August, 1958. For that purpose, they wanted people of the whole nation engaged in the making of iron and steel. They ordered people to build a lot of old-styled ovens, like in the kitchens of old houses, where there were open grounds for the ovens. In all other factories other than steel plants, a couple of ovens were set up. As to where to get the raw materials, they commanded people to take down all the steel doors, steel bars on windows, and steel fences, and to sell all their household things made of iron and steel, such as utensils. If people could have cut food with wooden knives, they would have ordered them to give up their steel knives. This disturbed production of other necessities and caused an economical mess. As a result, they declared on the 19th of December, 1958, that the total output of iron and steel was 11,080,000 tons, task victoriously completed, but more than 3,000,000 tons of steel from old styled ovens and 4,160,000 tons of iron from the same kind of ovens were all no good, all garbage. A great waste of money and materials and labor force. It was estimated that the loss was about 20,000,000,000 yuan of Chinese currency. A landmark in poor governance. But Mao was the emperor of the Red Dynasty.

This movement also affected students. Classes were assigned to build an old-style oven in a corner of the school yard. The steel blocks they produced looked like hard pieces of black bean curd, somewhat like the size of a brick. People called it Tofu steel brick.

Then the school authorities sent the students to a factory to help the workers to make such steel, so that the factory workers could go back to their normal production. There were some ovens already built on the open ground in the backyard of the factory, right in front of the canteen. Since the students came to help the factory making steel, the factory provided them with lunch gratis. The dishes were always a piece of meat and some vegetables, or eggs with vegetables. Everyone could only choose one dish. The rice was steamed in bowls, big ones and small ones. The girls always took small bowls and the boys usually had big bowls. Some strong boys who did heavier job took a big bowl and a small bowl, for they needed more nourishment.

How did they make the steel bricks? Some iron or steel pieces were put in the oven till they melted a little, not thoroughly melted, and stuck together. Then the piece was taken out and put on an iron anvil. One person tightly held the half-melted piece in long-handled vices on the anvil, and two other persons knocked on it each with a big hammer while the person holding it turned the piece round to shape it into a brick. The two persons hit the piece by turns while it was very hot. Even gloved hands could not stay long near it. The person holding it did not need to change hands, because he had long-handled vises and was a little farther from the hot piece. When the piece got somewhat cool and the shape was fixed, the job was deemed finished. This steel brick was put aside and they worked on the next one. There were more than one oven, and three persons were needed for the job from one oven. The students took turns to rest during the eight hours.

Then, what happened in the countryside? At first, the land reform policy of the Party was to take the arable land formerly owned by the wealthier classes and divide it among peasants. A few years later, the Party wanted the peasants to join so-called Cooperative Communes organized and led by the Party. That meant that the Party took back the land and organized it into Cooperative Communes. These Communes belonged to peasants collectively, in name, but as there were Party secretaries who managed the communes, it was really the Party's property. They could do anything they wanted, and peasants had no say in it. Even if the peasnts knew more about farming than the bureaucrats did.

Mao wanted to enlarge the cooperative commune into so-called People's Commune. On the first of July, 1958, the first People's Commune was established, merging 27 cooperative communes, with 9,360 families involved, in HeNan Province. Its official name was Chayashan Satellite People's Commune. The commune was really a basic local government. It governed almost everything in the district of the commune, from the agricultural production to people's daily life. It had public canteens, kindergartens, clinics, shops, and its own armed forces called militia instead of police.

As peasants no more had their own land and worked for the commune with very low pay, their productive enthusiasm was quenched. The Party owned later that it was a mistake, a wrong policy. In order to raise productivity, in 1985, a so-called professor and scientist Qian Xuesen, created a theory of "High Productivity," by calculation only, without any practical investigation. He was not an agronomist nor a Plant Physiologist, but a missile designer. He wanted to meet Mao's desire and invented such a theory. It was called "high productivity satellite." When Mao learned the theory, he gave instructions that all the communes had to carry out the theory. But the land could not yield so much as theoretically calculated. Therefore, false statistics was reported to the Party. From June to November, high production was reported thirty-nine times. The highest yield of wheat was 7,320 catties (catty = half a kilogram) a mu (15 mu = a hectare), that of corn 35,394 catties a mu, that of rice 130,434 catties a mu, and sweet potato 567,570 catties a mu, etc. Thus, people got the impression that everything said in newspapers, and on radios and TV stations in China under the leadership of the Party, were all lies. Possibly, Mao believed in all.

As it was reported that the peasants had produced so much grain, Mao and other Party leaders worried about what to do with so much grain. Mao said that peasants could eat to their full for free, and if Chinese people could not consume so much, they could give the surplus to the foreign people. They also wanted people in cities to organize people's communes. In every block, the Inhabitant Committee had to have a canteen so that the inhabitants could go there for meals, like in the communes in the countryside. But most of the city inhabitants did not go to eat in the canteens. They still cooked at home. So the city people's commune was a quick failure. Then Mao criticized himself, saying that he had listened to Qian, the missile specialist, as if he had no brains of his own. When Tian Jiaying, his secretary, asked him that as he had been a peasant himself, how he could not know that it was impossible to produce ten thousand catties a mu. It only showed that Mao had no knowledge of science.

Mao wanted to hurry into the "communist society" before his death to show that he did a great job to bring the communist society in the theory of Marx into reality. Therefore, he suggested Three Red Banners: the General Policy, the Great Leap Forward and People's commune. The General Policy was four words: Plentiful (quantity of products), Fast (productive process), Good (quality), and Saving (raw materials). Mao forced his ideas to be carried out, and as a result, the whole nation sank into economical plight. Then things became scarce, especially food. People in cities had to use limited coupons to buy all the necessities such as rice, flour, meat, eggs, cloth, cooking oil, sugar, cigarettes, matches, yarns of thread for sewing cloth, and even bath tissues. There were also coupons to buy cakes, biscuits, or anything made from rice or flour. If anyone went to a restaurant and east rice or noodle, he should give rice coupons besides paying money. The cashier's work was made a little complicated, who had to take in money as well as rice coupons. Coupons were distributed according to the number of persons in a family, and were given to the family every three months. At the beginning of every quarter, housewives were expecting the distribution of coupons to buy all the necessities needed for everyday life. The scarcity showed that the Three Red Banners ended in failure, too.

In July, 1959, the Party held a conference on Mt. Lu, on which Peng Dehuai, minister of National Defense Ministry, handed to Mao his "Ten Thousand Words Letter," to point out all mistakes made so far. But Mao refused to listen to him. On the contrary, Mao criticized Peng severely, and called Peng and his supporters an "Anti-Party Clique." They were removed from their official positions and jailed. But Chinese people respected them for their boldness to speak out the truth.

From 1959 to 1961, a serious famine broke out in China. Some report revealed that at least 3 billion people died from hunger. Many in the countryside ate grass and tree barks to maintain their lives. Another report calculated that people died between 4 billion and 6 billion in number. The Party denied that it was a famine, but named it as natural catastrophe. It really did not matter whatsoever name they used. Later, however, Liu Shaoqi, the chairman of so-called People's Republic of China, confessed that it was seven-tenth human responsibilities and three-tenth natural calamity. Even during the famine years, the Party still exported a lot of grain for foreign exchanges. In 1959 when lots of people were starved to death, 4,157,500 tons of grain were exported to Soviet Union and other socialist nations in east Europe for the purpose of getting help to develop military industry. Besides, in April, 1960, they gave 10,000 tons of rice to African countries and 15,000 tons of wheat to Albania, ignoring the famine that was killing their own people.

Shanghai is the largest city in China. Provisions were transported there from other regions in China. So no one died from hunger. People in big cities were just kept at the survival level. The Wu family bought flour ration and rice ration, which was twenty-five catties per person. They cooked rice into porridge, which needed less rice and more water, and made steamed buns with flour. At that time, an egg cost 50 fen (100 fen = one yuan, equivalent to 100 cents = one dollar) in black market. But they used cigarette coupons to change for eggs, as none in the family smoked. The person, who generally came from the countryside, exchanged eggs for cigarette coupons, and sold them to heavy smokers. The rice coupon had two kinds, local coupon and national coupon. Local rice coupon could only be used in the city, like in Shanghai. National rice coupon could be used throughout the country. It was because people had to travel, and they had to use national rice coupon to buy food in other places. Other coupons were all for local use only.

People in Shanghai, if they had family members, relatives, or even close friends, in Hong Kong, would get parcels shipped from there, such as canned cooking oil, packages of sugar, etc. If anyone received foreign currency from abroad, emitted by family members or relatives, he would get Foreign Money Coupons and could use them in a special store to buy good-quality furniture, bicycles, watches of good brand, etc., anything people could not get in ordinary stores. That special store in Shanghai was called Oversea Chinese Store. One had to show foreign money coupon as entrance ticket. This store was exclusive to people at large. The Wu family got such things from friends in Hong Kong.

In 1959, Genghua was still in senior middle school. The fourth son was in the junior middle school. Genghua made friends with two classmates, Zhang and Sima. Zhang's father was retired and mother was a housewife. They lived on fixed interests, too. Sima's father had returned from Japan and his mother was a Japanese woman. They spoke Japanese at home. The father had work and got income. The classmate Yang was not deemed a friend because in the anti-rightist movement, when Genghua had been criticized, he had accused Genghua of keeping contact with the "traitor" Bai, though he had also wanted to befriend Bai before he left for Germany. Zhang and Sima kept their mouths shut. The party was instructing people to put loyalty to country ahead of personal feelings, and to speak frankly about their friends and neighbors; but human nature dictates otherwise and the majority acted according to their hearts.

In the Great Leap Forward period, students in middle schools were told to write poems and sing songs of praise to the Party. The second son of Mr. Wu worked in Shanghai Diesel Engine Factory as a technician, and a girl technician there fell in love with him, but he did not like her. Once the girl called Mr. Wu's house seven times in one day, complaining and asking why the son ignored her. (All the private phones were taken away at the beginning of the Cultural Revolution. But the Wu family still had a phone at that time.) Later the family joked about it and gave the girl the nickname "Seven Calls." Somehow, in the end, the second son married the girl. They had a daughter and a son. There is a Chinese saying: If a girl wants to run after a boy, there lies between them only a piece of paper. (It means that it is easy for the girl to break through it and get the boy.) If a boy wants to run after a girl, there lies between them a cliff.

CHAPTER 10 – COPING WITH THE GREAT FAMINE

During the famine period, many people in Shanghai, if possible, applied for permanent permit to move to Hong Kong or Macao, the two closest exits to the international world and freedom. There was also a temporary permit to these two places. With a temporary permit, one had to return to the original place from which he left. With permanent permit, one did not need to return and could stay there forever. That was why people always applied for the permanent permit. Some people applied for passports to go to other countries, if they had family or relative relationship there. Quite a few people got permits and passports. Someone even stealthily ran across the border to Hong Kong or Macao at the risk of being shot dead or caught and sent to jail. There was still someone who swam across the sea to Hong Kong at the risk of being drowned.

In the summer of 1960, Genghua graduated from middle school. Before graduation, every student had to fill fifteen universities or colleges in the selection form. The teacher in charge of the class advised Genghua to fill in English major as his first choice, but Genghua thought that any kind of language studies could be finished outside university all by himself, why should he waste time to learn language program in a university? He always deemed himself as a language genius. He could write classical essays and classical poems, better than those majoring in Chinese literature in the universities. So he filled Biochemistry as his first choice. He wished to be a scientist. At that time he was too young to know how such things worked in communist China. Universities and colleges selected students based on their family background as well as the comments the teacher wrote in their personal files at that time.

Genghua did have a chance to be enrolled in Shanghai Conservatory of Music. One day when their singing group was practicing, a man came from the conservatory to their group to choose students who sang well. The man wanted Genghua to go to the conservatory to be enrolled in singing department. But he did not like the idea of being a professional singer, so he did not go. He had supreme confidence in his ability to do well on all sorts of tests or entrance exams.

However, the university authorities were not selecting students according to their marks, but according to what kind of family the student came from and the political status of the student. Only Party or Youth League members could take such an important major as biochemistry. Genghua had engaged in some disputes about political issues and his politics teacher had written him down for "reactionary thinking" in his personal file. This was no good for his future.

So Genghua did get good marks in the university entrance exams, but he only he won admission to the Liaoning Coal Mine Normal University, which was not even one that he had selected. Everyone else in his class was all accepted into whichever universities he or she desired. Liaoning is a province in the far northeast of China. Very cold. And coal mines are dangerous. So Genghua gave up the chance and chose to stay at home to take the examination again next year. But universities accepted students who only graduated in the current year, not in the last year. He did not know it, either. Accordingly, he had no chance the next year. His friends Zhang and Sima were enrolled respectively in East-China Textile Machinery Institute and Shanghai Foreign Languages Institute. He still kept in touch with each of them separately. Once when Genghua went to

Zhang's house, his parents told him that Zhang had gone to the US. His maternal uncle lived there and went through a lot of procedures to get him there to be enrolled in a university. Genghua and Zhang did not write to each other. But Genghua went to see his parents from time to time. He met Sima whenever Sima was free. Genghua now was free and happy as a lark every day.

The Wu family lived on fixed interests, which were not much. He wanted to find a job, but jobs were assigned by the local government, namely, the Street Committee. At that time many cadres had leftist thinking and hated those who did not need to work for living, those idlers they called them. However, if idlers could give them something, anything as gifts, as bribery, they would take every care of the idlers. But Mr. Wu and his wife were not flatterers by nature. A neighbor working as artist and living across the side lane, one house down, gave the policeman in charge of the block some of his paintings as the policeman liked Chinese paintings. But The Wu family did not even know it, though they had a box of old paintings. Genghua went to the Street Committee for jobs, but someone there said to him that he had to wait at home, and if there was a suitable job for him, they would notify him. They, nevertheless, never notified him. Maybe, there was never a suitable job for him. But what kind of job was deemed suitable to him? It was for the cadres in the Street Committee to decide for him. The strange thing was that the Party never owned that they had jobless people. They called those people idlers, and for students like Genghua, who just graduated from middle schools and had no chance to be enrolled in universities and had no work, they were called Social Youth. A weird nickname.

As Genghua graduated in years of famine and so many people were applying to go abroad, Mr. Wu got an idea that he could also apply for a permanent permit to Hong Kong where some friends of his had owed him some money. He wanted to get the money back since the government at that time was thirsty for foreign currency. He wanted Genghua to accompany him on the way as he was old and sick. His intention was to take the son to Hong Kong where he could find a job. At least one of his friends would give him a job in his company. So they both handed in their application forms and waited in expectation.

Mr. Wu wanted his reason for application more convincing so that he asked Mr. Chen, known in Wuxi, to come to write it for him as he had been a lawyer. Mr. Chen came in the morning. He wrote it and crossed it out and rewrote it, weighing every word he wanted to use. It took him two hours to finish. He was persuaded to stay for the potluck and chatted a little in the afternoon.

Probably in every society, there are certain people who enjoy seeing other people suffer, and seeing people fail in their endeavors. So they find ways to set up hurdles on other people's road in life.

There are ten districts in the city of Shanghai. The police precinct of Xuhui District, where Mr. Wu lived, had a department in charge of issuing permits to Hong Kong and Macao. In fact, the police precinct in every district had such a department. They had a reception room where people could go to inquire about their applications. As so many people were applying, they had to wait in line for quite some time. It seemed that there was someone in this department who did not want Mr. Wu to go to Hong Kong and did not approve their applications. But any applicant so denied had the right to apply again. So that someone thought of an idea to discourage their further application.

In the first floor room of the house lived a couple. The husband, Mr. Mao, was the brother of the primary school teacher who had taught Mr. Wu's sons. This Mr. Mao worked in a branch of the People's Bank and was versed in calculation, including calculation of his own benefits. One day this Mr. Mao came upstairs and talked to Mr. Wu. He made two requests: firstly, he had to be allowed to use the full bathroom upstairs, not just the half bathroom downstairs, and secondly, his present rent was too high for the room he lived in and had to be reduced.

Mr. Wu was capable of some calculation, too. He had a friend working in the housing department of another district. He asked him to come to Mr. Wu's home and explain a few things. What he explained was that since all rental houses now belonged to the government, and tenants paid their rent directly to the housing department, if Mr. Mao wished to have his rent reduced he would have to make his request to the housing department, not to Mr. Wu. As for the use of the full bathroom upstairs, a contract was signed when Mr. Mao moved in. If he wished to change the contract, he would have to sue Mr. Wu.

Then Mr. Mao went to Comrade Fan, a cadre of the block's housing branch under the housing department. Comrade Fan told Mr. Mao that the housing department rules maintained that all the bathrooms had to be available for use by all tenants in the same house. So Mr. Mao came to bring this news to Mr. Wu. Mr. Wu again consulted his friend and found that no such rule was written in the housing department regulations. Therefore, Mrs. Wu went to see Comrade Fan and asked him to show her to read the rule in black and white. Of course, he could not show the written rule. Mr. Wu decided to lock the upstairs bathroom.

Their dispute developed. Mr. Wu had no time to go to the police branch to fill out another form applying to go to Hong Kong. The quarrel between the Wu family and Mao family turned hot. One night Mao snuck upstairs to break open the lock. The Wu family persisted in their position that the Mao family could not use it, and changed the lock. Finally the quarrel turned rough, and Mrs. Mao hit the old grandma in the chest. Grandma spat blood and was sent to the hospital.

During the famine years, the government had wished to reduce the population to lessen the need for food. They allowed more people to go abroad than before, especially old people who could not contribution to building the country, or "the socialist construction," as they termed it. Seizing this opportunity, Mr. Wu handed in another application form. A few weeks later, he went to see Comrade Zhou, a leader in the police branch, and expressed his wish to go to Hong Kong on private business. Comrade Zhou nodded, and told him to wait at home. After another couple of weeks elapsed, one day the police branch sent for Mr. Wu and gave him a permanent permit for Hong Kong. But Genghua's application was not approved, though father and son had turned in their forms together. Therefore, Mr. Wu had to start on his long journey alone.

Mrs. Wu made the necessary preparations for her husband. Mr. Wu took a train, got through Customs and entered Hong Kong. It was November of 1960. Some friends of his came to meet him. One of them was Mr. Rong Meixin, who was the husband of the lady who had been named "Miss Shanghai," Xie Jiahua. The election of Miss Shanghai happened in 1946. Mr. Rong had voted for Miss Xie and married her later. Mr. Rong was also in the dye business. His main brand was Bear & Tiger, because in the Shanghai dialect the Chinese word "bear" sounded similar to his surname Rong. He add-ed the tiger because he thought of himself as a tiger in business. He earned a lot of money and bought a big house for his wife. Before the Communist Party came to Shanghai, he went to Hong Kong with his wife Xie. A far-sighted man, Mr. Rong later moved to New York City.

Another friend of Mr. Wu's was Mr. Wang Tingxin, who was famous due to a tragedy in his family. His son, Teddy Wang The Huei, was kidnapped and died, and a controversy broke out in Hong Kong as to about who should get the legacy he left. The case was won by his daughter-in-law, Nina Wang Kung Yu-Sum. It was in all the newspapers. Teddy Wang The Huei had been boyhood friends with Genghua and the second son of Mr. Wu. The fourth son of Mr. Wu was a bit younger and he could not play with the big boys, but he knew Teddy Wang. When he went to Hong Kong later, he had contacted with Teddy Wang.

Then Mr. Wu collected some money from his former debtors and opened a dye shop like the one in Shanghai, with another friend as a partner.

Long distance telephone calls were very expensive and no one had private telephone in those days, except high-ranking Party cadres. So Mr. Wu and his wife had to write letters to each other. Genghua kept applying to go to Hong Kong, now with the reason that he wanted to look after his father who was getting old, over sixty now. In the intervals between handing in an application and its denial, he started to learn English, learning thirty or forty new words every day. The next day, after reviewing the words he had memorized the previous day, he learned by heart another thirty or forty new words, in part from textbooks and in part from classic novels such as *Treasure Island.* He had a teacher named Mr. Li.

Genghua started to write compositions in English and gave them to Mr. Li for correction. As if Mr. Li did not like to correct compositions for learners, he introduced Genghua to a Mr. Fang, who had been an editor of the English newspaper "North China Daily News," which had been published in Shanghai before the Communist Party came. He owned a house at West Fuxing Road, twenty minutes walk from Genghua's home. He charged four yuan a month. The class met once a week. Five pupils in all. They sat around a round table. The book he taught was an old text book bought from the used book store. The book contained many famous essays, speeches and poems, and there were notes after every lesson. Mr. Fang not only knew English very well, his handwriting was beautiful, too. He had certainly lost in standing since the days when he had been an editor. In addition, he and his wife were both pious Christians. But now they could not go to church. They worshiped at home. Mr. Fang had a daughter who was a doctor, but worked in another city. His son was a violin student in the Shanghai Conservatory of Music.

Genghua continued to write English compositions and brought them to Mr. Fang for correction when he went to class. Genghua made friends with some of the pupils there, especially Liu, Ni, and a girl named Xu, and they would visit each other or get together once in a while. Genghua learned later that Miss Xu and he were distant relatives through father's side. Her family came from Ningpo, too.

Liu's father, an artist and painter, was labeled a "capped reactionary." This was a category of social offender invented for those whose devotion to the regime was so dubious they were deprived of the rights of citizenship. Mr. Liu was not allowed to go about town freely, much less to leave town. Whenever he needed to go out, for instance to go to hospital or a local clinic, he had to report to the police branch. If any of his friends came to see him, he would have had to report that to the police branch, too. But under such circumstances, no one came to visit him. Genghua was able to visit his son, because his son was a citizen. Once old Mr. Liu painted a turtle in mud, indicating that he was a turtle stuck in mud now. If this painting had been seen by any official and reported to the police, he would have been very severely criticized, and publicly. Liu's mother was a housewife. His elder brother was a middle school teacher married to an actress of the Shaoxing opera troupe. His younger brother tragically died at the age of ten by drowning in an artificial stream in the People's Park, almost in the center of the city of Shanghai. The family said that God had wanted him in heaven. His elder sister lived in Hong Kong and his younger sister was married to a worker and was pregnant when Genghua and Liu came to know each other. Once Genghua's mother asked old Mr. Liu to paint a picture of Avalokitesvara and asked a friend of Mr. Wu's to take it to him when he returned to Hong Kong so that her husband could worship this Buddha there.

Ni's father lived abroad, working on a ship, in charge of purchasing and supplies. His mother had never worked. He had three younger brothers. They all had jobs except this Ni. His brothers had very funny nicknames at home, Black Bushel, Ox, and Little Yak. Little Yak was talented in sculpture and some small pieces were displayed in their home. Of course, there was no way he could sell any of them. Ni liked to listen to the Voice of America, which was recognized as an enemy broadcast. If anyone was caught listening to it, he would have been arrested. Ni used a small radio and listened under his quilt. Anyway, it improved his English pronunciation.

Chapter 11 – Genghua and the Old Scholars

For almost two years they all went to class and enjoyed themselves. However, one day in spring of 1963, Mr. Fang told them that the Residents Committee of his block had forbade him to have private classes at home. He had to say goodbye to all his pupils, and the class was dismissed forever.

But the four friends still kept in contact with each other. Before long, Ni came to know a Mr. Shao, who was suffering from severe asthma and heart trouble. His grandfather had been the governor of Taiwan in Qing Dynasty, the last dynasty in the history of China. His wife came from the richest family in the area to the south of Yangtze River. He should have had a comfortable lifestyle, but now he had become poor and lived in one shabby room of a big house. He said that once he had inherited all the properties in his name, he had begun to spend money, never earned money. So his money diminished quickly. But he had been a famous person in the literary society of old Shanghai. After the Communist Party came to power, he was put in prison for some time. Now he did some translation for a publishing company and earned a pittance. He had studied in Cambridge, England. He was interested in poetry. So Ni introduced

Genghua to him. as Genghua loved poetry both in Chinese and in English.

Then Genghua would go to see Mr. Shao alone to talk about English poetry with him. He gradually became acquainted with meter and rhyme in English poetry. Once Ni and Genghua expressed their wish to learn English from him, but Mr. Shao said that he was too busy with translation and not healthy enough to have pupils. But he recommended to them a Mr. Wang, who had studied in Dublin University, Ireland. According to Mr. Shao, his English was very "substantial." So they went to see Mr. Wang with a note from Mr. Shao. It was in the autumn of the same year.

Mr. Wang lived in a very small room, with only a single bed, a desk and two chairs, leaving very little space to move about. He came from a banker's family. When he was in a senior middle school, he joined in a student parade against the central government of that time in Peking. It was early in the twentieth century. His father was afraid that he might bring trouble to the family and sent him to Dublin University, Ireland. He studied very hard and whenever he went to see a play by Shakespeare, he would learn the whole play by heart. As he watched the performance, he would recite all the dialogues, following the actors and actresses. Audience sitting next to him were surprised to hear him, and looked at him in admiration. At least, that was what he told Genghua. When he returned to China, he stayed in Shanghai instead of Peking. He worked in Shanghai Municipal Committee as an engineer. Now he was retired and his wife had died some years ago. He had a son working in Beijing as a government cadre.

Mr. Wang always had one pupil at a time. He charged one yuan for one hour every week. So Genghua and Ni came at different times. He already had a few other pupils. Then Ni introduced Miss Xu to him. And Genghua introduced Qian and Wei. Qian was the son of a friend of his father's. His sister lived in America and he was applying for the immigration into the US. Therefore, he wanted to learn English. Wei was the son of the Wu's family doctor, who owned a house of double room type with three storeys. Doctor Wei was a good diagnostician and learned from his own and from other doctors' experience; he did not depend on results from medical equipment.

Once when Genghua came to Mr. Wang's place, after the lesson, as no other pupils came, Mr. Wang told him a true sad story about his friend Mr. Chen, which went as follows:

Mr. Chen was the son of a rich merchant. His girlfriend was Miss Wen, who came from a wealthy family, too. Her father owned two factories. That year, Chen was twenty-four years of age. Shanghai had been occupied by the Japanese army for three years. One day, Chen took his girlfriend to a dance party. The host gave excellent entertainment to the guests. Plates were filled with all sorts of refreshments of both Chinese and Western styles. Cups gleamed with coffee and milk. When dancing was in recess, singing ensued, mixed with gleeful chatting and laughing. At dinner time, tables were loaded with dainties and plates heaped with delicacies. Wine in cups reflected the lamp light and ivory chopsticks clinked with silver dishes. Some played finger-guessing games and some made jokes. Dancing resumed after dinner. The party ended at midnight, the happy young people's shadows overlapping in the hustle and bustle. People bade each other farewell.

Chen left with his girlfriend. Just then, a taxi came slowly up. Chen signaled it to stop and asked for a ride home. They got into the back seat. There was a man in the passenger seat in the front. Chen thought that he had to be a friend of the driver, going for a ride, too. He didn't think that it was unusual and weird. The taxi sped forth. After a few turns on the way, it reached Consulate Road, toward east. Consulate Road is the present East Jinling Road. It was built in 1860. The French Consulate was located at the eastern end of the road, hence the name. The taxi went just in the opposite direction. Chen got scared and started to ask what was going on. When he asked again, he was told, "Shut up if you don't want to die." Then, all of a sudden, the taxi stopped as it reached the Bund. They pushed Chen out and accelerated across the Garden Bridge with the girl still inside. The taxi parked outside Xinya Hotel, which was then a military club for officers of the Japanese army. The girl was shut up in a room and lived in disgrace. She thought of Chen day and night in endless tears.

Chen witnessed the taxi speeding off and could not chase it. He shouted after it in vain and had to return home, weeping bitterly. That night, he was sleepless. Early in the morning, he rushed to the home of the girl and told her parents about it. The girl's household cried. Her father sent out his people in quest of her everywhere, but in vain. Chen himself also searched for her all over the city. He sank into great agony, knitting his brows all day long. He neglected his sleep and food, his clothes becoming loose by degrees day in and day out. His mother felt sorry for and sympathized with him. She advised him to marry another girl, but he would not listen and kept up his quest of her all the more desperately. He behaved like a mad man. Thus, a couple of years elapsed. No one knew where the girl was.

After Japan's surrender, the girl at last returned home and told her family all about her sufferings. When Chen learned of her return, he hurried to her home, in hopes of expressing his lovesickness, but the girl refused to see him, sending down her maid with the words, "My sullied body doesn't deserve your love any more. Marry elsewhere and think of me no longer." Chen persisted in seeing her, saying, "Your sufferings only deserve pity and sympathy. It's not your fault. My love for you is still the same. Please, come down and talk to me." He accused her of forgetting their vows. He waited in their living room for three days. The girl was greatly touched and finally came down to meet him. In due course, they united in holy matrimony. But Mr. Wang did not say whether the couple still lived or not. Perhaps he had lost touch with them.

Genghua used the novel *Pride and Prejudice* by Jane Austin as a textbook. He also practiced essay writing under Mr. Wang. Genghua also found other novels to read, such as *Gulliver's Travel, A Tale of Two Cities, Wuthering Heights, Jane Eyre, Ivanhoe, Vicar of Wakefield, Pilgrim's Progress, The Canterbury Tales, Robinson Crusoe, Of Human Bondage, The Old Man and The Sea, Gone With the Wind, Sister Carrie, The Sea-Wolf, Tom Sawyer,* etc., and some famous plays, such as *Pygmalion* by Bernard Shaw, *Merchant of Venice, Hamlet, The Twelve Nights,* etc., by Shake-speare. And also some translated novels from French, Russian, and other foreign languages, such as *The Count of Monte Cristo* and *Three Musketeers* by Alexandre Dumas, *War and Peace* by Leo Tolstoy, *The Red and the Black* by Stendhal, *Crime and Punishment* by Dostoyevsky, *Don Quixote* by Cervantes, and *The Divine Comedy* by Dante, etc. Then also *Sketch Book* by Washington Irving and *Golden Treasury,* a po-etry collection, and poems by Keats, Yeats, Shelley, Wordsworth, Browning, Shakespeare, and Longfellow.

Once he met Wang Keyi, a translator of the novel *Pride and Preju-dice* into Chinese. A good version of that novel. Although Wang Keyi had graduated from the English Department of Fudan University, he still felt that he could learn more from Mr. Wang. He committed suicide in the so-called Cultural Revolution.

As for Liu, one of the four friends, he had been recommended by a woman cadre working in a police station, whom his brother knew, to teach English in a junior middle school, and seldom had free time to mix with other three. But he would visit Genghua on weekends and sometimes to discuss with some English language problems in his teaching. Once he took Genghua to the Zhu family in his neigh-borhood. The Zhu family consisted of the father, who worked in a bike factory he used to own, the mother, the maternal grandmother, and a daughter. They had a single house, with a small garden in the front. There was, in one corner of the garden, a tiny pond with a tiny bridge over it, so tiny that only one child could stand on it, with some flowers and a few trees around it. The father now worked in the factory as an engineer and liked to take photos. Color photos were not yet common. He printed color photos at home, using the bathroom as the dark room. The grandma had owned a graveyard, one significant enough that Genghua had heard of it. Liu was intro-ducing Genghua to the family because the parents wanted someone to teach their daughter English, as she was branded a "social youth." Denied the privilege of applying to university, and having no job, she was an "idle member of society." This was an awkward reality for a regime that claimed to have eliminated unemployment. Her parents did not wish to let their daughter fritter away her precious time. Genghua agreed and came with Liu to Zhu's house.

The parents and the grandma liked Genghua very much and almost looked upon him as a future husband for the girl. Although Genghua had reached the age for marriage, his conditions would not allow him to entertain the idea. First, he had no job. How could he support the family if he got married? Besides, he was still applying to go to Hong Kong. If he got the permit to go, he would have to leave a wife behind. And the police would not let his wife apply and go to Hong Kong soon. That was for certain. Then they would have to live separately for who knows how many years, just as many husbands and wives were doing at that time in China. What was more, there were plenty of truly beautiful girls around, while Miss Zhu was neither beautiful nor clever enough to live independently. She had grown up under the protection of her parents like a chick under the wings of the hen. So she was not the right type of the girl for Genghua. Anyway, Genghua taught her English without charge for a couple of months. Then, Genghua thought that, as Mr. Wang needed money, he should introduce him here to teach the girl English. The mother agreed and one day Genghua brought Mr. Wang to the family. From then on, Mr. Wang rode a bike there once every week. Genghua continued to visit from time to time, just as a friend of the family.

The Zhu family was still interested in Genghua, however, even though they could not directly say that they hoped he and their daughter would get together. Moreover, they wanted to know more about Genghua, that is, about his family background and finance. So they thought of a strategy. One day when Genghua came to see them, the mother said to him that she wanted to introduce a girl to him, to which Genghua agreed. They would meet in the Zhus' house. On the day when Genghua came, he saw a pretty girl there. He thought that it must be the girl they wanted to introduce to him. So they started a general conversation. A short time later, according to tradition, the boy had to take the girl aside somewhere so that they could talk freely about any matters of concern.

They found a nearby tearoom and had some refreshments. Genghua paid for it, of course; a tradition, too. After they finished eating, the girl wanted to go home. When Genghua asked her when they would meet again, the girl said that she would decide later and he could get information from the Zhu family. So they parted. A few days later, Genghua went to the Zhu family's house. After some small talk, the mother got to the point. The parents wanted to know how much money Genghua's father had in Hong Kong and how much fixed interest they could get here in Shanghai. Genghua was not happy to be asked such awkward questions. So he made no reply and diverted their conversation elsewhere.

When Genghua met Liu next time, he told him about the questions Mrs. Zhu had asked. Liu said that Genghua should tell them that his father had only one Hong Kong dollar there and two yuan here, to see their reaction. But Genghua could not really say that; Liu was only joking. And the whole matter was dropped.

One day when Genghua was walking in the street, he suddenly noticed a note stuck on a lamp post. Since all the newspapers were controlled by the Party, no private ads could be posted in them, even if one wanted to pay for it, and so people started posting announcements on walls or lamp posts. The one Genghua read said, Shanghai Amateur Choir wants more singers. The address was underneath. Genghua loved to sing, so he went there. After a test, he was accepted. He sang tenor. When the whole house still belonged to the Wu family, Genghua used to practice singing and he would climb the scale in the living room when he was there alone, and managed to make the lamp hanging from the ceiling echo with a vibrating sound. Sometimes he went to the house of a young man in the neighborhood, another so-called social youth. He had a piano at home, and he told Genghua that he could reach high C at the top of his voice.

The Shanghai Amateur Choir had rehearsal once a week and sometimes performed with Shanghai Choir in public concerts. Shanghai Choir was a professional one belonging to the government. It meant that the Choir was under the leadership of the Party while the amateur choir was independent, organized by individual singers voluntarily. All singers in the professional choir had graduated from music colleges. The two choirs performed once in Shanghai Concert Hall and once in Culture Square, which could hold an audience of ten thousand.

Genghua lost his singing voice after the Cultural Revolution because he ceased singing altogether during that period, and his singing muscles degenerated. What he loved to sing, Western songs or old songs, he could not sing for fear of criticism. And what he was allowed to sing, songs in praise of the Party, he was not willing to sing.

Genghua had reached an age to enjoy true love, but there were no girls to be found with an intellectual inclination who would be a good match for him. He poured his emotions into poetry.

Chapter 12 – Tours in West-Suburb Park & to Suzhou City

Mr. Wang had about ten pupils. They did not know each other because they came separately. Only a certain pupil would meet another before or after his time. Once Mr. Wang asked all his pupils to have a gathering in a park, part of which was a zoo. It was called the West Suburb Park. All the pupils liked the idea. As those pupils were all so-called social youth, they could meet any time any day. So they chose a weekday, when the park would not be crowded. It was spring, warm and sunny. A good day for touring.

They met at the park gate, and then, went in together. Everyone one bought his own ticket. A pupil called Zhang bought the ticket for Mr. Wang. They strolled around, joking, laughing and taking photos. They went to the zoo part, visiting the animals. Monkeys were always the favorites with visitors, especially with children. Some were trained to play with balls. There was a king among a group of monkeys, who had a right to eat first when food was served. When the old king died, there would be a fight among the other male monkeys to decide who would be the next king, just like in the human world. This lends further credence to the theory that humans are evolved from monkeys, as Chinese students were told in biology class. The elephants were playing soccer ball, kicking it to and fro. Their trunk can pick up things as tiny as a needle. In hot days, they use their trunks to suck in water from a small pool especially dug for them, and spray water on their bodies to get cool. The pandas were asleep. Since pandas are found only in certain parts of China, they are highly valued. The Chinese government occasionally makes a gift of pandas as one of its diplomatic tools. A giraffe ran nimbly to the tall fence to look at the visitors. It is said that a giraffe can jump as high as six meters, but it cannot issue any sound as it does not have vocal cords. A chimpanzee stood on his forelimbs with his back against the wall of the cage. The students jested that it was exercising Kungfu. It is said that a chimpanzee can be trained to do some of the human duties. A hippo was so impolite as to make dung publicly and the bad odor was spreading just as they reached its place, so they all ran away as fast as their legs could carry them. The colorful goldfish were pleasant to scrutinize. Their tails looked like gauze skirts spreading out. There were many varieties, including one with a transparent bubble that grows around the eye and another variety with its eyes placed so that they always look upwards.

At noon, they took lunch in the park cafeteria. There was a specialty that day: a tiger had died and its meat was cooked for sale. That was a bit much for the youngsters and they just ordered ordinary dishes. Zhang again paid for Mr. Wang. His father lived in Hong Kong and owned a company. Zhang had plenty of pocket money from his father, and he liked to make sure everyone knew it. After lunch, they sauntered along the footpaths and came to a shady arbor. They took a rest and someone suggested playing a guessing game. The game went like this: One person went outside the arbor, out of hearing range. Others decided on, say, two Chinese words. Then the person outside came in and could ask two questions of anyone he chose. The first one he put the question to had to use the first of the two words in his answer. The second one had to use the second word in his reply. From this, the person who was guessing should try to tell the others what were the two words. In the first round, the two words were the two words of the person's given name. He would never guess that his own name was what he wanted. After a few round of the game, they walked to somewhere else in the park. They left for separate homes at four p.m.

Now all the pupils got to know one another well that their activity circle enlarged. Zhang was one of them, and afterwards, Genghua was invited to go to his home to play a kind of Chinese chess, sometimes. Ni was a good-looking man, like a gentleman. Zhang said to Mr. Wang that Ni was a nice man to befriend. But one day when Zhang went to Ni's home in his absence and saw that Ni slept in an attic in a shabby house in an area called the "down corner" in Shanghai, he said to Mr. Wang that since Ni lived in such poor environment, he would not have a gentlemanly family education. It was not suitable to make friends with him. Mr. Wang passed this comment of Zhang's to Genghua, so that Genghua came to understand Zhang's character better and he began to see him less often.

Miss Xu lived in Shanghai with her grandpa. Her father had died and her mother and brother lived in Suzhou, a tourist center. They had a house there. Once when she declared that she would go there to live with her mother for a while, Ni got an idea. He suggested to Genghua and Zhang that they could travel to Suzhou for sightseeing. Miss Xu said that they could go with her and stay in her house, saving money for lodging. Then they could return by themselves. She would stay longer. So the four of them took the train there. When they arrived in Suzhou, they took a bus to the stop close to her house. Her mother gave them a big supper. The three men slept in one room, on one big bed, for the night.

Next morning, Miss Xu took them round for sightseeing. The first place they went was the zoo, where there was a big turtle worth seeing. But the turtle was nowhere to be seen in the pond. Maybe, it was shy before so many strangers and hid at the bottom. Only they saw a brown deer with white spots all over the body looking like plum blossoms. Then they went to Lion Grove Garden famous for its grottoes. They went through cave after cave, sometimes got on top of the grottoes. It was a nice place to play hide-and-seek. Then they continued to the Humble Administration Garden. Even a slight drizzle did not quench their enthusiasm for sightseeing. It was typical of Suzhou parks, with lawns, trees of many sorts, pavilions, and little ponds. Out of this garden, they took a horse-drawn carriage round the city for a while.

Next day they went to Tianping Hill. It's cloudy that day. On the mid-slope there was a tearoom with a pond outside the railings. Water from a spring snaked into it. The spring water was used to make tea. Climbing up further, one had to go through a very marrow path between two cliffs. The sky looked like a thin thread. Hence, the name of the spot: One Thread Sky. Out of the path, there was a forest of stone pillars with the upside ends very sharp. On top of the hill there was a large flat rock. If clambering on it, one could command a wide long view all around.

Lingyan Hill had been a palace of King Wu in the War Period of the Seven Kingdoms. The renowned beauty Xishi, wife of the king, lived there. Many dynasties later, it was turned to a temple. But now the monks were all dismissed to be peasants. The Communist Party does not believe in anything but Marxism and the gun. There was a corridor called Clog-Sounding Corridor. The legend stated that the corridor was made with vacant pottery vats under wooden boards in Xishi's time. When one walked on it wearing clogs, a sound was heard echoing from the empty vats underneath.

Tiger Hill was of great interest to tourists. A legend had it that when the king of the Wu kingdom died, his tomb was built in this hill. After three days of the burial, a white tiger appeared on top of the hill. Hence, the name of the Tiger Hill. A famous scene was the Sword Pond. It was an artificial pond, five meters deep. A legend said that the King Wu had several best swords made and when he died, his son put those swords in his tomb. The pond was the entrance to his tomb, to the swords and great treasure inside. Many kings or lords of power thereafter had tried to dig into the tomb and lay their hands to the famous swords and great treasure, but all in failure. After three days, Genghua, Ni and Zhang went back to Shanghai, to their respective homes. They bought a pack of cards in Suzhou and played some game on the train.

The fourth son of the Wu family graduated from middle school, but he did not enter any colleges, and so became a social youth, too. Genghua stopped applying, and instead, his mother and brother sent in application forms. It was better that way. If Genghua went there alone, how could he look after his father and work at the same time? If his mother and brother went there, the brother could work and mother could look after father. Then Genghua went to the Street Committee often to ask for a job. But he was denied application and denied job, too. Someone wanted to see what would happen to the family when at the end of seven years no more fixed interests could be collected.

Then Mao family living in the first floor room was arranged to move to somewhere else. It must be that the someone behind the scene did not want things to go too far, out of control. At that time there were no empty houses for anyone to move in. The one who wanted to move had to look for a place he liked and exchanged his place with the one living in the place he liked to move to on condition that the person liked his place, too. It was called housing exchange, which had to be done through the housing department for approval, if each liked the housing of the other.

The new family having moved in comprised the father, three sons and three daughters. The father had owned a small flour mill, and was of course a capitalist. He was retired now and the mother died. The first son worked in some other city, only came to visit the family on main holidays like Spring Festival. The second son was married to a girl with Italian origin. They both were the so-called social youth, i.e., without job. The third son worked in a factory. The first and second daughters were married and lived with their husbands somewhere else. The third daughter was a middle school student. Soon after they moved in, the second son got a job teaching in a primary school. Then he and his wife got a room somewhere and moved into it and lived separately from the father. That might very probably be the conditions that the family agreed to move into such a small space of one room for so many family members.

When Genghua went to the Street Committee to argue why the second son of the family downstairs got a job so soon after moving in, and he was not given any job even if he often came to ask for one, none there answered his question, and he still had no job. Meanwhile, he studied English harder.

CHAPTER 13 – TALENT STILL FLOURISHES IN THE SHADE

Now Liu came to Genghua's home less and less. Every time he came, he would ask Genghua some questions about English he was teaching. Then he would boast of his relationship with his colleague, a son of a high-rank cadre. He would have been a social and political climber. But his family condition would not allow it. So he liked to know someone on there, or at least someone whose father was perching there. Once when he came, he told Genghua that an old man needed someone to help him with compiling a book. The old man, Mr. Ju, was versed in Chinese classics and known as a knowledgeable scholar in the circle of Chinese classics. When he knew that Mao Zedong liked the poetry of Liu Yuxi, a poet of Tang Dynasty, he began to compile the poems by that poet into a book. The famous couplet from a poem by him was:

Thousands of sails pass by a wrecked ship;
Myriads of trees flourish beside a blighted one.

It was said that Mao liked this couplet very much. It had some philosophical idea in it. Anyway, Mr. Ju needed someone to copy his manuscript onto special paper for a manuscript. That someone had to have learned Chinese classics so that he would not make many mistakes when copying. So Liu took Genghua to see Mr. Ju, who appreciated Genghua's classical training. Genghua visited Mr. Ju three times a week thereafter. Mr. Ju promised Genghua that he would try to recommend him to Shanghai Ancient Books Publishing House he worked for. Moreover, during the process of assisting Mr. Ju with the compilation of the book, Genghua learned a lot and Mr. Ju helped him in his further studies of Chinese classics. The book was finished in a few months and was published soon afterwards.

One day Genghua went to see Mr. Shao, the sick translator. He told Genghua that the day he had received his inheritance, he began to sell things, such as antiques, and spent the money. He produced a small box. There were two seals of semi-precious stone with crimson spots in them, the color of the spots looking like that of the blood of the rooster. This sort of stone was named "Rooster Blood Stone," very expensive. The larger the spots on the stone, the more precious the stone was. The two stones in Mr. Shao's possession were good ones. But at that time, such things were under-valued. Mr. Shao knew that Genghua was acquainted with an old man who collected antiques, such as stone seals, paintings, and porcelain vases. So Mr. Shao asked Genghua to take these two stones to him. He needed only fifty yuan. Genghua had to take the box and promised to try.

At home, he consulted his mother, who considered it improper to do. Therefore, the mother gave Genghua fifty yuan and wanted him to give the money to Mr. Shao and return the stones to him. Accordingly, after a few days, Genghua went to see Mr. Shao again and did what he was told by his mother. Mr. Shao took back the box and accepted the money. He said that he counted the money as borrowed. But Genghua knew that he could never repay it. Anyway, he did not care. It was a donation.

Genghua kept having lessons from Mr. Wang. One day Mr. Wang found Genghua not so strong and introduced him to another Mr. Wang, who could teach him Taiji. So Genghua went to see Taiji Wang (for distinguishing purpose). Taiji Wang was in his eighties now. His calligraphy was very good and he had been a Chinese language teacher in a senior middle school before his retirement.

His wife died long ago and now lived with his sister in seventies. Genghua began to learn Taiji and came to know more people. A Mr. Tan in fifties was the grandson of the famous Tan Yankai, a general of the revolutionary army against Qing Dynasty. He was jobless, too, and sold whatever his father left him for living. He was also acquainted with Mr. Shao. A Mr. Xu was also in fifties, and did not work. Supposedly he lived on family inheritance or some other income. Once Genghua visited him and he talked about his neighbors, the Chen brothers, who were learning English all by themselves. They lived in a big house with a large courtyard in the front. Their father died early and they now lived with the mother. Their elder sister lived in Hong Kong and they were applying to go there. Then Mr. Xu took Genghua to see the Chen brothers, the big Chen and little Chen, both jobless. They lived on fixed interests, too. Their father had been a capitalist. The little Chen was a social youth, and already married. He liked to buy English dictionaries whenever one was on the bookstore shelves. He would read through the dictionary and make comparison with others. So he had a wide vocabulary. He even knew the word fylfot, which is the sign on Nazi flag while the swastika denotes a Chinese pattern. They are a little different in shape. But American people sometimes mistook the Chinese pattern for the sign on the Nazi's flag and this caused some misunderstanding. It is because they are confused with the two words fylfot and swastika in meaning. Big Chen had graduated from a university and assigned to work somewhere else other than Shanghai. So he refused to go and chose to stay at home, jobless. He was defined an idler, not a social youth. During the conversation both sides learned that their fathers had been in the same trade before and must have known each other. At least they knew someone in common in Hong Kong, a relative on both sides. So Genghua went to see the brothers sometimes. Once a friend asked Genghua to translate an article in a foreign magazine about computer science from English into Chinese. Genghua found difficulties with it. Even if he found meaning of every word he had not learned in the dictionary, he could still not make out what a sentence meant. It needed the background knowledge of computer. So Genghua took the magazine to Big Chen, who knew something about computers. He could also build a radio set just by buying all the parts from a store.

Once Genghua felt his lower back uncomfortable. It was not pain, but something we Chinese called a feeling of "sour" in the muscle. When he went to Taiji Wang, he mentioned it. Taiji Wang offered to treat it with hie *chi*. A good taiji exerciser or teacher can emit *chi* from his hands into the body of others. That was what Taiji Wang was doing to Genghua. Taiji Wang put his right hand on the affected spot on the lower back of Genghua, who felt a warmth quickly filtering into his body through his thick clothes. It was winter and he wore a pullover and a cotton coat. As the warmth filtered into his waist section, his uncomfortable feeling was gone right away. Taiji Wang said that Genghua was a good conductor of *chi*. One of his neighbors was a nonconductor. When he tried his *chi* on him, he did not feel anything.

His next door neighbor was a very old man with a little beard growing on his chin, like a goatee. He had been a mayor of a small town under the Qing Dynasty. It seemed that the Party had never bothered any officials of the Qing Dynasty. It might be that the Qing Dynasty was too far away from the present regime in history and they had no immediate conflict of interests. So the old man lived in peace. He could read faces. One day when he met Genghua, he said that Genghua had a hook between his left eye and the bridge of his nose. He had known a person with such a hook, and once on a tram, he met a friend who helped him a lot in his career. He concluded that Genghua would have such a chance. So Genghua awaited his chance ever since, but it never turned up.

Another woman in fifties was a party secretary in charge of the Textile Bureau in Shanghai, but she had some chronic disease and had a long sick leave. That was why she had time to come to exercise Taiji. Her husband worked in another city. She had three daughters and a son, the youngest one. The eldest daughter worked in a factory and two other daughters had gone to the countryside, answering the call of the Party. After the Cultural Revolution, when universities enrolled students once more, her second daughter entered East China Normal University in Shanghai. Her third daughter got married in some other place. After they got acquainted for some months, Secretary Zhang, as Genghua called her, invited Genghua to her home and asked him to teach his son English. But it lasted only for a short time as the son had other plans.

Secretary Zhang came one day to visit Genghua's mother. They had a pleasant conversation. Mrs. Wu asked her about the rule that the bathroom should be used by all the tenants in the same house, as she must better understand the policy of the Party. Secretary Zhang said that she never heard of such a policy. So when she went to talk to Comrade Fan in the housing office, she told him that even a Party secretary did not know of such a policy. Comrade Fan was shocked to hear it and did not say anything more.

Once the mother of the Zhu family wanted Genghua to take two old paintings to show to Mr. Shao and ask him if they were genuine or fake, as there are so many fake Chinese antiques in the market. When he took the paintings to see Mr. Shao, he saw another man there, Mr. Pang, as introduced to him, whose family was renowned for its antiques collection. Mr. Shao and Mr. Pang looked at the paintings and decided that they were fakes. When Genghua returned the paintings to the mother, she was disappointed.

One day Liu came again and took Genghua to the house of a friend of his, the Xue family. The mother of the family was the daughter of Liu Hongsheng, a famous capitalist in old China, who had sold coal for a foreign company and had opened a match factory later. The old man had died by then. Now the father and mother of Xue family were in the US. The second son was there, too, who had been a middle school classmate of Liu. Liu got to know the other family members through his classmate, the second son. That day, they had a party at home. So Liu took Genghua there for some fun. Then Genghua came to know the eldest son Xue Lijin, who had had a job in the northeast of China, but resigned from the work and came back to Shanghai, jobless now. He was applying to go to the US, as his parents lived there. So Genghua and he became friends. Xue family had eight children, but two of them died early. The father had been an architect and built two houses for the family on the same site, one bigger and one smaller. The small one was unoccupied. All lived in the big one. They liked to have guests coming as their house was so big. Then the sixth son, Xue Lita, came to see Genghua and wanted to learn English from him. He just asked questions when he had difficulties in learning. So he got to know Genghua's younger brother Kunhua because they were close in age. Now he was known as Little Xue, and his eldest brother as Big Xue. The seventh was a sister and the eighth was the youngest son.

One day Little Xue saw Genghua's Chinese handwriting and liked it. He did not know that Genghua had practiced Chinese calligraphy when younger. Next time when he came he brought some cards and asked Genghua to write some Chinese characters on them using only the ball pen, not Chinese brush. It was easier for him to imitate. So he came oftener for that purpose and brought cards he had practiced on for Genghua to correct.

Genghua was acquainted with a fat man through his stepbrother, the second son of Mr. Wu. The man lived just next door to the former residence of Sun Yat-sen on Xiangshan Road. His family, father, mother, and brother, all lived in Hong Kong. When Genghua asked him why he did not to go there, he confessed that the family had valuable antiques in Shanghai and he had to stay here to watch over them. The Communist Party did not permit any antique over a hundred years to go outside China, out of their control. They looked upon all these valuable things as theirs though in individual possession at present. The man believed in Buddhism and never wanted to marry. He told Genghua an interesting story about a silver statuette. One day he went past the curiosity shop. Every shop belonged to the government now. He went in to look round, without any intention to buy anything. Then his eyes fell on a silver statuette, the label saying it was the statuette of God Guan. However, it did not look like God Guan from the description in the history books. God Guan should wear armor and grew long beard. His nickname was "Beautiful Beard Man." This statuette had no beard at all and had a hunchback. The price of it was one-hundred-eighty yuan, not expensive. He went home and looked for data in all the books he could get. To his surprise, the statuette matched the description of the emperor Qianlong of Qing Dynasty. It was worth a lot more than the price. So he took the money and went there to buy it. Luckily for him, the statuette was still there. He made a worthy investment.

On one visit to the fat man, Genghua met a Mr. Hu, there, whose family was now in Australia. He lived in Shanghai alone. He and Genghua had a pleasant chat and he invited Genghua to his home to see the tropical fishes he kept. He had many sorts of tropical fishes, some beautiful, some transparent, some in neon color. A black kind was called Black Maria, the scavenger of the glass tank to keep fishes in. His aim of life was to own a farm for livestock in Australia. He was not married yet. What he thought about marriage was just what Genghua had thought before, no wish to live separately with wife. Both husband and wife being approved were very difficult at that time. But Genghua had changed his mind. If his mother and brother could go to Hong Kong, he would marry in Shanghai, because it was impossible for him to get the approval.

Friends of both brothers of the Wu family often had potluck. The fourth son, Kunhua, had some former classmates who often came. One of them was Feng, a classmate in the senior middle school. Feng was also a social youth. Feng had three younger brothers and a younger stepsister. His father married a younger girl of Feng's age. The girl was the daughter of their former woman servant. So the brothers despised their stepmother. The younger sister was born from the stepmother. All these members of Feng family were jobless. They depended on the grandpa, who had a brother in Hong Kong. He sent money to the grandpa every month because the grandpa had been the partner to the brother in a company they both set up. The money was really the dividend. The grandma never worked. There were quite a few families whose members were all jobless. When Feng came and Genghua did not go out, the three boys would play cards for fun. Cards were permitted to play, and mahjong was not. Another classmate of the fourth son in the primary school, Zhao, came often, too. He worked in Shanghai Foreign Trade Bureau. Most of those mentioned so far would play some kind of role later in the life of the Wu family in the so-called Cultural Revolution movement.

Since Mr. Wu had left for Hong Kong, the family lost touch with almost all his friends. But if Mrs. Wu needed help she could go to see any of the former family friends. However, there was never any need for such help. One person still kept in touch with Mrs. Wu: a niece, Mrs. Shen, on Mr. Wu's side. Mrs. Shen was the daughter of the eldest brother of Mr. Wu, who was the youngest of several siblings and the only one still living. The niece was about as old as Mrs. Wu. She had five children including a son who lived in Hong Kong. When he went to Hong Kong in the early fifties, he got a job through the recommendation of Mr. Wu, his granduncle. Her fourth son worked in a factory, too, and lived at home with his mother. Genghua often went to see her and she sometimes came to visit.

Another occasional contact was Youfeng, the niece of Mr. Wu's first wife. Another friend of Mrs. Wu was the second wife of a certain Mr. Chen, who was not only much older than she, he was much older than Mr. Wu. He had a factory in Hangzhou and had now retired at home in Shanghai. Mr. and Mrs. Wu were like the god-parents of the son, the "dry" mother and "dry" father. The idea may occur from the idea of "wet nurse." As such a "mother" never feeds the "dry" son any milk of her own, the mother is dry, not wet. This kind of relationship indicates a very close feeling between two families. Mr. Chen had some retirement money from his former factory. The money was remitted to him from Hangzhou. As he lived a long life, the leaders in the factory thought that he might already have died and his wife might have cheated them by receiving the money in his name. Therefore, they sent someone to Shanghai to see whether the old man was still alive. When the person came into their room, he witnessed Mr. Chen sitting on a chair, sipping tea. He went back and reported to the leaders, who had to keep remitting him his retirement money. Mr. Chen died at ninety-two. The other Mr. Chen, a former lawyer returning from Indonesia and acquainted with Mr. Wu in Wuxi City, came no more since Mr. Wu went to Hong Kong.

One day, unexpectedly, Comrade Yao, the policeman in charge of this block, came to see Mrs. Wu. He just asked some general questions about her husband, and then gazed at a painting on the wall. He asked some questions about the painting, showing an obvious interest in it. If Mrs. Wu took the hint and gave him the painting, it might help them gain approval of their application. But Mrs. Wu was an honest person. She was afraid that it might be deemed bribery, and bribing a policeman was a crime. So she said nothing and did nothing. After a while, Comrade Yao left. Months later, she was told that a woman next lane gave Comrade Yao many gifts and she had already received the permit to go to Hong Kong.

Chapter 14 – The Cultural Revolution Deals Capitalists the Final Blow

During the so-called natural disaster, as 30 million people were starved to death, the national economy got worse and worse. Therefore, Mao was forced to recede to the background, and Liu Shaoqi stepped into the foreground, helped by Deng, the secretary general of the central committee of the Communist Party. Of course, such a very ambitious person as Mao would never, of his own accord, give up the political power he had enjoyed so far and now stand backstage watching others perform on the political stage right under his nose. No, he would never allow it. This was the reason of the occurrence of the Cultural Revolution he was scheming in his great mind.

In January, 1962, at a meeting of 7,000 people, Mao criticized himself for the mistakes he had committed, having made a mess of the national economy. Liu said then that it was three-tenth natural calamity and seven-tenth human error. But in August of the same year, on the meeting at Beidai River, Mao insisted in his theory of class fight, which was the main danger of the present society. Mao thought that there was still the possibility of revisionism taking the upper hand, which meant the revival of capitalism. In the later development of the events, one could see that Mao laid a time bomb in theory to turn the tables for his benefits. This was his basic theory to wage the Cultural Revolution in future. Liu and Deng could never see the red lights—the approaching danger. Both were no equal rivals to Mao.

The Cultural Revolution was certainly unprecedented in the history of China. If Mao had his IQ tested, it should be very high. If his scheme for the movement went a bit amiss, the result would be different. He might never retrieve his power, or the whole country would be in civil war. His scheme was accurate, though he never cared how many people would die in the culture revolution. He was a person cruel at heart. When his third wife, Yang Kaihui, had been arrested by Chiang Kai-shek's government and killed later, he didn't do anything to rescue her and then married another woman. He sent his son to the Korean War, who died there.

In February, 1963, the central committee of the Party decided on another political movement, proposed by Mao, imaginably. This was, indeed, Mao's strategy to retrieve his lost power. No one could see through him at the time. Liu, the chairman of the nation then, was of course the leader of the movement. As usual, Liu sent out work teams to the countryside for the movement. Liu thought that the target of this movement was still the common people as the previous movements did. The work teams made a mess there as they really had no idea whom they should target.

In December, 1964, at a meeting of the central committee of the Party, Mao said that it was wrong to aim at the common people. The target should be the cadres. Of course, Mao meant more than that this time. So Liu made self-criticism. A trap Mao set for him to fall in. Then in January, 1965, the central committee agreed with Mao that the target of this movement should be those in power within the Party, who were persisting in going the capitalist road. At that time, no one could guess who were those targeted in power. But Mao had a certain goal in his mind. Another theoretical trap. It was based on this theory that Mao was the right person going the socialist road, and any other persons who held different opinions from Mao should be those going on the capitalist road. The worst thing was that all other leaders of the Party agreed to this theory, making Mao always standing on the correct summit. Mao could never be wrong theoretically. It was called the fight between the two roads: the socialist road and the capitalist road. As Mao declared himself and was also accepted as the representative of going the socialist road, Liu was, of course, deemed the representative of going the capitalist road. Going on capitalist road was wrong, according to Mao's theory, which was accepted by others. Liu already lost there. His tragic end was sealed even before the beginning of the Cultural Revolution since others were all got confused by Mao's theory and didn't know how to contradict him.

However, Mao still let Liu lead this movement, as a Chinese saying goes, "If you want to get, you must give first." Mao had read a lot of Chinese history books and was versed in all the stratagems in power redemption. Liu, as usual, sent out work teams again. Statistics showed that in the region of Changde Town, in HuNan Province, 331 persons were criticized, among whom 21 were beaten, 65 bound hand and foot, 3 hung up, and 42 forced to kneel on the ground. In a suburb of Beijing, 40 people committed suicide. Only this time, the target was the lowest cadres in the countryside, not common people anymore, as Mao had planned to use common people as his chessmen. Pawns are powerful when they get in a certain position. The red guards were his chessmen.

Meantime, Mao traveled all over the country. He talked secretly with some important generals and wanted to get their support. He always believed in gun. If he could get those holding the gun to support him, he could go on with his plan. Otherwise, he would stay backstage for the rest of his life. From the Chinese history, a conclusion is true: the wise can always gain the upper hand of the fool. Mao, the wise. Liu, the fool. Among all the generals, two of them were the most important ones, Lin Biao, minister of defense ministry then, and Xu Shiyou, commander of the army covering the area of Nanking and Shanghai. With their support, Mao was sure of his final victory. However, the procedures of the process must be taken very carefully. He could not have a step amiss.

At that time, most of those in power in local governments were supporters of Liu and Deng. How to seize power from them was a problem. If most of the local government leaders supported Mao, he had no need to start the Cultural Revolution. Since the situation was otherwise, Mao had to get his ball rolling. However, Mao plotted wisely and nicely. Mao liked to control consensus first so that he could say anything using public opinion against his political enemies. So he commenced his plot in that field.

Mao wanted his wife, Jiang Qing, to help him. Mao married Jiang Qing while he still had his legal wife, He Zizhen, sister of Marshal He Long. At that time Mao's legal wife was in the Soviet Union for treatment of presumed mental disease. Mao and Jiang held a banquet in a big cave in YanAn. It was December 21, 1938. Jiang was twenty-four years old then, twenty-one years younger than Mao. The original name of Jiang Qing had been Li Yunhe, and her stage name was Lanping. She changed her name to Jiang Qing when she went to YanAn. She had been married before to Tang Na, also a movie star. A story went at that time about three couples who had their simple wedding ceremony held under the moonlight before the Liuhe Pagoda, in Hangzhou. The three couples were Jiang Qing and Tang Na, Ye Luqian and Zhao Dan, Du Xiaojuan and Gu Eryi. All were movie actors. The witness to their marriage was Shen Junru, a man of letters. After their wedding, Jiang Qing always quarreled with Tang Na. Their relationship worsened and Tang Na was ready to kill himself by drinking poison just sixty days after their marriage.

In 1937, Jiang Qing lived together with Zhang Ming, the director of the movie. Then she put a notice on the newspapers to declare that she had separated with Tang Na. After the outbreak of the Sino-Japanese War, Jiang Qing went to YanAn. Later Tang Na went to Paris, France and married Anna in 1952. He died in 1988 of some disease. In the Cultural Revolution, most of the actors who had worked with Jiang Qing were put into prison as Jiang Qing feared that they would spread work of her history as a third class movie actress, which, in her opinion, would make her lose face. Many of them died in jail. Luckily for Tang Na, he lived in France at that time.

On the wedding day of Mao and Jiang, the Japanese airplanes bombarded the town. They were safe in the cave. Just like the marriage between Chiang Kai-shek and Song Meiling, known as Madame Chiang, the marriage of Mao and Jiang was based on three conditions, which were not put either by Mao, or by Jiang, but by the political bureau of the Communist Party. The first condition was that as Mao still had his legal wife, Jiang should not declare herself as Mao's wife in public [Does it mean that she is a concubine?]. The second was that her duties were only to look after Mao in his daily life and for his health problems. The third was that she should not join in political activities or interfere with the Party affairs in the twenty years thereafter. It was because Jiang had been a third-class movie star in Shanghai. People did not think highly of movie stars at that time. Let alone a third-class one. It was probably that she was aware that she could never become a first-class star that she gave up her career in filmdom and went to YanAn to seek political future.

The three conditions Madame Chiang put were those: firstly, Chiang must become a Christian by baptism; secondly, Madame Chiang won't have children with Chiang; thirdly, Madame Chiang won't take any government office, she acted in public only as the personal secretary of Chiang. So different the conditions were from those of the other couple.

As Jiang Qing had learned to sing Beijing opera, she began in the area of Beijing opera reform, which happened between 1964 and 1966, after she issued an article "Talk on Revolution of Beijing Opera." It gave her a bridge over which she could take part in the political movements later. When she had married Mao, the Party had passed a document that she had been forbidden to be involved in politics. The opera reform only involved culture. That's why, maybe, the revolution called culture revolution, an actual political revolution in disguise. So none in the Party had any objection. Generally Beijing opera was about old stories. The reform made it into modern stories. The ones known in China were "Red Lantern," etc.

Ballet was reformed, too. The famous ones were the "Red Detachment of Women" and the "White-haired Girl."

On the tenth day of November, 1965, Mao let his wife, Jiang Qing, instruct Yao Wenyuan in Shanghai to write an article criticizing the new historical play "Dismissal of Hairui from Office," published in Wenhui Daily. It was because nothing could appear in newspapers in Beijing at the time. All officials there were Liu's men. The article said that the play wanted to redress the case of Peng Dehuai, because Hairui was the defense minister in Ming Dynasty equivalent to Peng before his dismissal. This play was written by Wu Han, a vice mayor of Beijing. He became the first official Mao wanted to get rid of, which would be a breakthrough into Liu's circle.

To support Wu Han, Peng Zhen, mayor of Beijing, organized a "five-person Cultural Revolution group," approved by Liu, Deng and Zhou Enlai, the premier of the State Council, intending to limit the criticism within the culture, not into politics. But Mao would not allow it.

On the 16th of May, 1966, on the meeting of the political bureau of the Party, a document, approved by Mao, was passed, known as "5.16 Notice," which was officially deemed the actual beginning of the so-called Proletarian Cultural Revolution. At the same time the "Central Cultural Revolution Group" was organized to replace the "five-person Cultural Revolution group." And Peng Zhen, Wu Han, and others in Beijing government were out of office. On the eighth of May, Lin Biao, the minister of the defense ministry at the time, said that Chairman Mao was a genius, every word he said was truth, nothing but truth, and a sentence from him was worth ten thousand sentences from others. This began the "Personal Worship" the nation over. Anyone said anything disrespectful to Mao, let alone against Mao, would be defined as a reactionary and put in prison. For that reason many innocent people became prisoners during the Cultural Revolution. Ridiculous stories were circulated. A person killed a cat and was jailed because the Chinese word for cat had the same pronunciation as Mao. The person killing a cat was deemed to have the intention to kill Mao. Someone accidentally threw a stone, which hit the picture of Mao hanging on the wall, and he was deemed a reactionary. A person walked in a park and felt tired. He saw a bench, which was dirty from the rain of last night. He put the newspaper he had just bought on the bench and sat on it. He was reported and arrested because there was a picture of Mao on the newspaper. The personal worship of Mao developed to such a degree in the Cultural Revolution.

Why should Lin Biao set up Mao as the object of the so-called "Personal Worship"? It had to be another tactics of Mao. The fact was so clear that those supporting Mao were much fewer than those supporting Liu and Deng. Mao, through Lin Biao, set up himself as the object of "Personal Worship" like a god being worshiped so that no one dared to oppose him. He could be always at the upper hand. Then the slogan of "Four Greats" about Mao appeared: Great Guide, Great Leader, Great Commander, Great Helmsman." Then Lin Biao, or someone else in his name, invented a style of dance, called Loyalty Dance. Generally the dancers held a card board with the word *loyalty* written on it.

Mao's wife, Jiang Qing, had been also an actress before she had gone to YanAn and married Mao. She originally lived in Shandong Province. There she was enrolled in Shandong Beijing Opera Institute. Later when she took part in some activities against Japan, she caught the attention of the local government and had to escape secretly to Shanghai. She joined the Left-Wing Drama Union, acting in some plays for revolution. It was said that when she acted in dramas she was okay, but when she was in movies, she was no good. When she was the wife of Mao, she was ashamed of her history as a star and did not want people to be aware of it, much less talk about it. Anyone who mentioned or even hinted at it would be put in prison, too. That was why many famous actors and actresses who had worked with her before were persecuted during the movement and many of them died in prison.

On the 25th of May, Nie, a woman Party leader in Beijing University, together with other six men, put up a so-called Big Word Paper, criticizing the Party committee of Beijing University and the municipal Party committee of Beijing City. At that time Mao was in

Hangzhou. When he was reported about it, he praised it, calling it the first Marxist-Leninist Big Word Paper in the country. On the same day, an editorial appeared on People Daily, calling upon ordinary people to join in the movement, to down all authorities.

On the 29th, the first group of Red Guards was organized in the subsidiary middle school of Qinghua University. The chaos developed fast. Students in many middle schools and universities rose to oppose the leadership of the Party there. Quite a few university principals were criticized. Seeing this, Liu sent out work teams in an attempt to control the situation. The work teams made 10,211 students the rightists, and 2,591 teachers the reactionaries.

On the 18th of July, Mao returned to Beijing. On the 24th, Mao held a meeting, criticizing Liu and Deng for sending out work teams. Liu confessed that he did not know how to lead the Cultural Revolution movement. Deng said that it was like an old revolutionary meeting with a new problem. That was where Mao set the snare to let them fall in. Accordingly, Mao took over the leadership as Liu and Deng did not know what to do. Even if Liu and Deng had not sent out work teams and did something else, Mao would, at any rate, find faults with them easily. It always happened in the struggle for political power in the Chinese history. All the same, the result would be for Liu and Deng to be out of power. The goal of the Cultural Revolution. Mao's scheme. Now Mao was back in power. It looked like that Liu and Deng were not driven out of power, but like that they were willing to give up the power to Mao as they did not know how to wage the Cultural Revolution. A real wise and best move of Mao, so easily to take over the power.

Mao supported the Red Guards. On the fifth of August, Mao wrote a Big Word Paper, titled as "Gun Down Headquarters—my big word paper." Mao meant that there was a "capitalist headquarters" in the Party, implying to Liu and Deng, who were out of power. Then Lin Biao was made the vice chairman of the Party, because he supported Mao to get the power back from Liu and Deng.

At the end of May, Red Guards developed on a large scale. On the thirteenth of June, the Central Committee of the Party and the State Council issued a notification that the entrance examination for the university was postponed for half a year. On the eighteenth, the editorial of People Daily said that the Cultural Revolution must be thoroughly carried out and the education system must be thoroughly reformed. The entrance examination system had to be stopped. Therefore, for more than ten years, no new students were enrolled in universities, and for many years, no classes for students in schools. Thus appeared a gap of education and knowledge between the old generation and the young generation. The young generation did not have enough education and enough knowledge. The Chinese culture in a general sense degenerated. Then what were the students doing? They were all taking part in the Cultural Revolution. Students in universities and middle schools formed red guards of their own. Primary school students stayed at home.

The red guards began to travel all over the country to instigate riot. They did not need to buy tickets either on trains or buses. That was the Party's decision. All they needed was an armband with the words Red Guards on it. It was easy to make and get. So other people, who were not students, seized this chance to travel for free all over the nation for sightseeing.

The whole country got into chaos. That's what Mao wanted to retrieve power from so many Liu's local government supporters. So Mao wanted the red guards to "destroy four old things," which were old thought, old culture, old tradition, and old custom. But it was not easy to define these. So everywhere the red guards went, they burned the old books published hundreds of years ago, the old paintings even by famous painters, and broke curios and relics. They destroyed old wooden shop signs and replaced them with paper ones written in new names. They even proposed to change the name of Shanghai into "July-First City," which Mao disapproved.

Why the red guards wanted to change Shanghai into July-First City was because the Party declared that the 1st of July, 1921, was the birthday of the Chinese Communist Party in Shanghai. But data on Internet revealed that it was established in August, 1920, under the instruction of the Soviet Communist Party. In April that year, the Communist International sent Grigori Voitinsky to China. In May, he found Chen Duxiu, forty-two then, to contact some revolutionary young men in other cities for the establishment of Chinese Communist Party, which was founded in August, 1920. Why the Chinese Party wanted to change their birthday to the 1st of July, 1921, was that it might have two reasons. One was that they wanted to cover the fact that the Communist International had a finger in it. The other was that the Party did have a meeting in Shanghai and Mao attended it so that they could say that Mao was one of the founders to make Mao look better. But the meeting was on the twenty-third, not on the first. Anyway, the Chinese Communist Party did not even give a correct day for their own birthday. How can we believe the narrations in the Party's history written by themselves?

The red guards went to private houses and ransacked and destroyed or took away all the valuable personal belongings. They even beat people to death. Statistics showed that in one month from 18th of August, 1966, in Beijing, 114,000 families were ransacked, and 85,198 individuals were driven to where they came from. From 23rd of August to the 8th of September, in Shanghai, 84,222 families were openly robbed. And in Tianjin City, 12,000 families were in the same disaster. Another statistics showed that during August and September, in Beijing only, the red guards got 103,000 taels of gold, equivalent to 5.7 tons, 345,200 taels of silver, 55,000,000 yuan Chinese paper currency, and 613,600 curios. In Shanghai, between the twenty-third of August and the eighth of September, besides large quantity of gold, silver and gems, etc., they got 3,340,000 US dollars and other foreign currencies worth 3,300,000 Chinese currency, 2,400,000 yuan of silver coins and 3,700,000,000 yuan of Chinese currency. A Party document confessed that even before that, the red guards already got 1,180,000 taels of gold, equivalent to 65 tons. That was really the aim of "destroy four old things." Mao and the Party wanted, in such a name, to rob people of their valuables. A broad daylight robbery! The robbed could not resist, nor even report to the police. The robbery was lawful, supported by the Communist Party and Mao. What was the use of laws in such a country? It was the final financial blow to the Chinese national capitalists. After that, they had nothing valuable worth to be taken away by the Party. They were safe now, as poor as a lazy squirrel with nothing in store for winter. The pillaging action affected those who had something worth a little money, but who were not the capitalists.

And many antiques were destroyed, worth billions. From the ninth day of November, 1966, to the seventh day of December, during less than a month, more than 6,000 articles of curio, more than 2,700 volumes of ancient edition, more than 900 rolls of paintings and calligraphy by famous ancient people, and more than 1,000 stone tablets, being destroyed. Who should be responsible for all the loss?

As to death rate during the red terrorism, the official statistics showed that only in Beijing, the capital city, 1.700 people were beaten to death. A massacre took place in Daxing Town outside Beijing and during three days, 325 persons were killed by cruel means, including some buried alive. Those who made suicide reached 200,000. In the whole period of the Cultural Revolution, the estimate of the death rate in the whole country was between 2,000,000 and 7,000,000, one percent of the whole population in China at that time.

In Shanghai, the red guards of Shanghai Museum went to all the collectors on their list to take all the curios to the museum, they said, for the sake of protect them, or the red guards from Beijing might destroy them. Some collectors even called the museum, asking it to send their red guards to their homes and take their curios away. Fortune sometimes means misfortune.

Other things happened in Shanghai during the red guards movement. At first, their action was only limited in the streets, destroying old shop signs. When they saw some women wearing high-heeled or pointed shoes, they would force them to take off and they would cut through them with scissors they seemed always carrying with them. They called it capitalist life style, included in the four old things. Once some red guards saw a girl wearing trousers or jeans. They thought it was a sign of the capitalist life style and forced the girl to take them off, and the girl had to run home in her underwear. They laughed after her.

Then when they heard what their fellow red guards did in Beijing, they started to attack private houses, too. Mostly they went to big houses, generally belonging to the capitalists. Some stayed in one big house for months, eating their canned food and chocolate in store. Some embezzled gold and silver articles and diamond rings. Others took away the interesting novels for their own enjoyment. The stupid ones they were deemed. Some of the capitalists were forced to kneel on the ground and beaten or abused. Lots of red guards went to Canton and tried to break past the border sentinels to rush into Hong Kong. They declared that they wanted to make revolution there, but were stopped by the Chinese army.

What happened to the Wu family? The houses in their lane were not big enough to attract the red guards from Beijing. Lucky for them. But it seemed the secret instructions of the Party that every capitalist home should be ransacked and valuables taken, however, in an organized way. No beating allowed. All the factories and stores organized their own red guards for that purpose. They went to the houses of the capitalists and took all their valuables. None would be missing on their list. As thoroughly as if a bedbug affected house was being cleaned.

As Mr. Wu was not in Shanghai and Mrs. Wu had never worked, it seemed that no concerned red guards would come to their home. But don't be happy too early. The second son of Mr. Wu worked in Shanghai Diesel Engine Factory. Through this relationship, the red guards from that factory came to visit the Wu family one evening. Mrs. Wu welcomed them in, since she could not refuse them. She had better use a welcome attitude. She gave them all the valuables of her own accord. So they did not ransack the place. They made a list of all the things they took and gave Mrs. Wu a copy. They left 200 yuan cash, 50 for each of them, the mother, the grandma, two sons without jobs. It was intended to cover their expenses for one month. They said that the government would decide what to do with the things at the end of the movement and they would get back to the Wu family shortly. But the Party estimated wrong. The movement lasted much longer than they originally planned. When Mrs. Wu was putting things back in order, she found an old IOU paper for two big gold bars. She mailed it to her husband in Hong Kong. Mr. Wu told her in reply that he had found the man and already got the money back, and so the IOU paper was no use now.

Then the red guards from the housing department came. They were welcomed, too. They came to force the Wu family to give back the second floor room to the housing department. And they took away all the furniture in that room and also the rest of the cash after they left 60 yuan for them, 15 for each. So far so good. No one could argue with red guards.

At the end of one month, Mrs. Wu went to the housing department to ask to be given back the rest of the cash for living, as surely the Party's policy would not let anyone starve in such a great city as Shanghai. She was told to ask her husband for money. So Mrs. Wu had to write to her husband. Mr. Wu then remitted 200 Hong Kong dollars every month, equivalent to a little more than 80 yuan, at the exchange rate at that time. Eighty yuan was enough for a family of four. The prices of major things were: rice at 12.9 fen(cent)/per catty, wheat at 9 fen/per catty, pork at 72 fen/per catty, chicken eggs at 63 fen/per catty, cabbage at 4 fen/per catty, pepper at 10 fen/per catty, coal ball (coal powder made into fuel for ovens) at 0.4/per catty, and firewood at 0.3 fen/per catty. The lowest pay at that time was 18 yuan a month. A higher level was 36 yuan a month.

Chapter 15 – Rebels Seize Power at the Local Level & Armed Fighting Begins the Nation Over

All the professors in universities and old teachers in middle schools were criticized or even beaten. Some professors were forced to crawl on the college sports grounds. Some were made stand for long hours in a bowing posture with both arms stretching straight behind, looking like an airplane. Some were ordered to bow before the picture of Mao for hours, too. In the Shanghai Conservatory of Music, the professors were forced to slap each other's faces in public. Never say that the Chinese people are not inventive. Since olden times, they have invented a lot of new torture equipment and styles. A standing cage was one of them. Any offender would be put inside with his head on the top of it, the neck in a small hole so that he could not move his head down into the cage. He had to keep in a standing position for how long he was sentenced to be. It was a trivial torment. For a prisoner, if he rejected to confess his crime the government official wanted him to confess, two thick wooden sticks would be put on his forelegs, one above and one under, with ropes on both ends. When the ropes were tightened, the pressure on the forelegs through the wooden sticks inflicted pain to the prisoner. The tighter the ropes were, the acuter the pain grew, till the prisoner fainted. For women, small sticks were used between her fingers, with the same effect on her. Another invention was to use an iron piece, made hot in the fire, then put on the chest of the prisoner. His skin on that part would be burned. No one can imagine the pain this torment caused without experience.

Yang, the classmate of Genghua in the middle school, openly criticized his parents, to show that he was loyal to the Party and always listened to the Party. Whatever the Party called upon him to do, he would obey, even to criticize his own parents. He would do whatever for his own future. Later, his parents killed themselves at home by opening gas stove without lighting it. For that reason, Genghua despised this classmate and never got in touch with him ever since.

Then, the target of the Cultural Revolution changed to the authorities of the local governments, under Mao's instruction. Mao thought that most of them were supporters of Liu and Deng. Therefore, so-called rebels rose and attacked the local government leaders. They seized power from the leaders and organized so-called revolutionary committees to replace the local governments.

Now the Cultural Revolution was on the power-seizing stage, which was really what Mao aimed at. It began with a movement targeting the petty cadres, really a false move of Mao to set up a snare for Liu; then it went to a stage to openly criticize a play to get rid of some important supporters of Liu in the capital Beijing; then it developed to the red guards stage to cause chaos in the country; then in the chaos, it got to the power seizing stage. It was the critical stage. If successful, smoothly, the last stage would be easy to tide over. The last stage was to put all the supporters of Mao in the local governments after getting rid of all Liu's supporters. The Cultural Revolution would thus end as planned by Mao. On this critical stage, if Chiang Kai-shek had ordered his army to attack the mainland, no one could tell what would be the future of China. But the stupid Chiang Kai-shek let the opportunity go like sands through his fingers.

Many rebellious groups were organized and fought each other to vie for taking over the power. Generally, at first, they got into a debate. At that time, people all over the country were learning The Little Red Book. Every time people wanted to say something, anything, they had to quote something from the Little Red Book first. Even when anyone was to write a self-criticism paper, he had to begin with a quotation from it. So when a debate began between two groups, the debaters had to quote from the Little Red Book to prove that what they were saying was in accordance with Mao's instruction. Thus neither side could overcome the other, as each was equally legitimate. It was called "Quotation Battle" since both sides used Mao's quotations to prove they were the right side. Debates often continued in a fight. But it seemed that quotations from the Little Red Book contradicted each other, or how could the opposite groups both cite from it?

The rebels among workers in Shanghai called their organization as Shanghai Worker Revolutionary Rebellious Headquarters. The commander-in-chief of this headquarters was Pan Guoping, a young worker from a factory. The famous Wang Hongwen was, at the beginning, the vice commander-in-chief, who was a Party member and a cadre of the lowest rank. On the 3rd of January, 1967, Zhang Chunqiao and Yao Wenyuan came back to Shanghai from Beijing and supported Wang Hongwen to seize power from Shanghai municipal authorities. Pan, being too young, was out of power, and was only made a member of the revolutionary committee. This event was called "January Storm," which caused the power-seizing action to develop to the whole nation. That was what Mao desired.

On the 6th of May, 1967, the leftists pro the Communist Party in Hong Kong, began a riot against Hong Kong government. The riot started with strike and demonstration, and developed to assassinations, bombing and gun fight. Luckily, it ended in October. Fifty-two people died, including ten policemen. 1,167 bombs exploded.

Almost everywhere in the country, rebels had benefit conflicts among themselves and they formed different groups and fought one another. Some, supported by the army, got guns. So gun fight began.

Once, even tanks appeared in the streets. The most serious fights were those:

From the twenty-sixth of February to the fifth of March, 1967, in XiNing Town of Qinghai Province, T55 tanks appeared in the streets and 822 persons died and 1,355 persons wounded. From the second to the twenty-fifth of August, 1967, in Yichun Town of Heilongjiang Province, 37 government buildings were destroyed and two military camps were gunned down in cannonade. 1,944 persons died and 1,806 persons wounded. From August to November, the rebels in Huaihua Town of HuNan Province occupied some labor-reform farms and factories and resisted the attack of the army. 37,700 persons died and wounded, including 430 military men. The death was 13,300. From June, 1967, to March, 1968, in Yibin Town of Sichuan Province, more than 170,000 people joined in the fight, including two army regiments. 43,800 persons died and wounded, the death was 21,100. From October, 1967, to the end of May, 1969, in Inner Mongolia, 56,200 persons were killed, and over 377,000 persons imprisoned, and over 3,550,000 involved, one fourth of the population of Inner Mongolia. From April to July, 1968, in Nanning Town of Guuangxi Province, 22 battles were fought. Over 101,000 persons died, and 74,000 people wounded. From December 1968, to February 1969, in eight ammunition factories in Baoji area of Shaanxi Province, out of 70,000 staff, over 45,400 workers were judged as reactionaries and 297 among them were executed, which caused the rebellion. Tanks, armored cars, cannons, and fire-throwers were used. Over 13,300 persons died, including some government leaders. Later, Mao and the Party strictly forbade this and the fight gradually subsided in August, 1968, and no more fight after 1969.

Supposing, under the most serious riotous circumstances, if Chiang Kai-shek sent his army to land on the mainland, the rebellious groups, who failed in power-seizing actions, would probably go to Chiang Kai-shek's army for support. Even Party members would do so for their own interests. Don't thing that Party members are always loyal to the Party. Many Party members are opportunists. They join in the Party for benefits or for the hope of becoming a cadre. A cadre would surely get benefits easily. And look at the facts that many upright Party members are imprisoned for their criticisms of the Party. Zhang Zhixin, a woman Party member, was killed by the Gang of Four, Jiang Qing, Wang Hongwen, Zhang Chunqiao and Yao Wenyuan, for criticizing the wrong-doings of the Party. For fear that she might shout out something unfavorable to the them, her throat was cut when she was taken to the execution site.

But no gun fights broke out in Shanghai. The army here was under strict control. The largest event was the fight in Shanghai Diesel Engine Factory, which was located in the northeast part of Shanghai and had ten thousand people working in it. At the beginning of the rebellious period, there were two groups in the factory, one called the East Red group consisting of Party members and cadres, the other called United Headquarters group consisting of workers and other staff. At first, United Headquarters group seized power and was in the leadership of the factory, but East Red group wanted to take over the leadership as they thought themselves to be the Party members and cadres and should be the leaders of the factory. Then fight began between the two groups. When Wang Hongwen became a leader of Shanghai, he supported the East Red group as he was also a Part member and a cadre. United Headquarters group rejected to give up the leadership.

On the fourth of August, 1967, Wang Hongwen sent ten thousand people to attack the United Headquarters group in the factory, and the vanguards were the trained firefighters. He did not at least dare to send army or police force there. The United Headquarters group defended the factory with only three thousand people. The weapons both sides used were mainly axes and steel bars. The defenders also used some glass bottles containing materials easily catching fire and big nuts to shoot from giant rubber bands.

Wang Hongwen acted as the commander and ten thousand people surrounded the factory. Finally the attackers used crawler crane to knock down the gate and rushed in. Every man captive got a good beating. Thousands of captives with blood all over walked between the attackers, singing the Internationale, into prison vans. Those who were injured seriously and could not walk were thrown into vans. The women were treated a little better. The next day, the members who had not been in the factory that day were arrested one by one. The second son of Mr. Wu was also a member of United Headquarters group. Only he was not in factory that day. Hearing that they wanted to arrest him, he went to hide in the house of his father-in-law. He returned to the factory when things cooled down a little. So he did not get a beating, as beatings were forbidden later. During the fight, thousands of people were hurt on both sides altogether. No one died, as no guns were used.

In all those days during the transfer of power, Genghua often went to read the "big character" posters (dazibao) that individuals were posting all over the walls and shop windows in the streets, revealing information most people generally did not know, compromising statements about the behavior and activities of the central leaders, complaints and observations that expressed the people's dissatisfaction. Very embarrassing for those responsible for maintaining the image of a unified nation.

Many jobless men also organized some rebellious groups and went to the Street Committee. They did not seize power from the authorities there. They just waited there and if any factory or store or anywhere sent in a notice to hire someone, one of them would put in his own name and use the seal to stamp on the paper. He took the paper and went to, say, the factory to work. He at last got a job this way. The authorities there did not dare to prevent him, afraid that all jobless people would get angry and beat them.

Genghua heard that Zhang, another social youth, had joined a rebellious group and was a leader, but some days later, he quit it, fearful that he might be accused of some minor crime and be put in prison afterwards, which would certainly affect his application to Hong Kong. His chief aim was to go to Hong Kong, to get a job.

Some middle school students, as there was no class for them, just fooled away their time by fighting each other for trifling reasons, or bullying other boys. One family had four sons who always bullied the other families in the neighborhood. No one had so many sons to fight them. But another family had four daughters. One would think that four daughters were no match for four sons in fight. But each of the daughters knew had some boys as friends. If each of the girls asked her male friends to fight for her, there should be around ten boys. So the four sons did not dare to bully this family.

The Wu family felt particularly vulnerable and often felt afraid that someone would send someone to do harm to them. Sometimes some boys in the neighborhood wanted to challenge the younger brother to a fight in public. One day, Feng, a middle school classmate of the fourth son, came unexpectedly. They had not met often recently. The fourth son welcomed him. He brought with him another young man with a red band on his left arm, which meant that he was at least a member of some rebellious group. At that time rebellious group was known as those who would fight or beat people for no reason. His appearance served as a warning to the boys in the neighborhood. Feng called him Little Jin.

Next time Little Jin came without Feng. He brought his younger brother with him. He wanted his brother to stay at Wu's home for the whole day. The brother had hit a boy's head with a brick and made it bleed in fighting. Little Jin thought that if his brother hid here, no one could find him, if the parents of the bleeding boy reported to the police. Meantime, he would go to smooth the matter as he was a leader in a rebellious group and had a little power. During his long stay, he talked about some adventures of the wild boys. One of the boys he knew was put in prison for fighting. When he came out, he said that the food in jail was unimaginably bad, but also not enough. When he was so hungry, he had to eat toothpaste. Poor boy. In the evening, Little Jin came and said that everything was okay now. He went with his brother, leaving his words behind that if anytime the Wu family needed his help, he would do his best.

Chapter 16 – The Wu Family Retreats during the Cultural Revolution

A couple of months after the Wu family was forced to give up the second floor room, a new family moved in, consisting of the parents, two daughters and two sons. Then the elder daughter got a job in a factory. The younger daughter graduated in 1969. Middle school students who graduated in 1968 and 1969 had no jobs assigned to them. They all had to go to the countryside to live and work with peasants. The Party called this receiving "re-education" from the peasants. But in the Party's theory, the peasant class represented backward productivity. They had backward thoughts. How could those with backward thoughts re-educate the students who had been indoctrinated by the Party for twelve years? No one could answer this question, not even the Party itself. (Although it certainly opened the eyes of spoiled urban youth to find out for themselves how primitive, tough, and limited real life was, out in the hinterlands.) This was mainly an excuse to drive part of the population out of the cities, to alleviate some of the shortages of supplies. People in cities should not be starved to death. It would create a very bad public image. People in the countryside did not matter so much, and 30 million people died of hunger without making the news. The Communist government would not take any political pressure at the time that happened. In fact, as the universities stopped enrolling new students, and as there were not many job opportunities for all the students, the Party had to create some kind of excuses to drive those students to the countryside to try their own chances of survival or to make them maintain the lowest life level there; it was better than leaving them to starve, as in famine years, in the cities. This movement was literally called "Up to the mountain and down to the countryside," because some remote peasant villages were high in the mountains.

The youngest girl in the Wang family, on the ground floor, graduated in 1968. But she did not go anywhere, just stayed at home with some medical excuse. She was jobless, too. But her status was different from that of the social youth. There wasn't even any special term for this kind of social status. The Wu family called her a '68 graduate.

A mournful day came. One morning Mrs. Wu found that her old mother had not gotten up yet. Generally she would rise before others and start the preparation for the day, like kindling the stove and cooking the breakfast. When Mrs. Wu went to her small room to see what had happened to her, she found that the old woman had died in her sleep at the age of eighty-one. Accordingly, they notified the other daughter in Suzhou. Soon the funeral was over and the body burned. The box with ashes was left on a shelf in the building of a public graveyard. The rule was that after the period of five years the box had to be removed by the family, or it would be thrown away. So at the end of five years the second daughter came from Suzhou and took the box with her. When she returned to Suzhou, she found a peasant outside of town and gave him some money, asking him to bury the box deep in the fields just out beyond his house.

Then Genghua moved to sleep in the small room. He seemed to feel the warmth of his grandmother's presence. One night before he went to sleep, he prayed that the grandma could tell him in his dream what his future would be. He could clearly remember what happened in his dream. That night, he felt in his dream that a cold feeling washed over him as he lay in bed, just like the description of a ghost appearing in ancient books, and then his grandma came in through the closed door. He asked her about his future, and his grandma answered him with the word Ningpo. When Genghua woke up, he thought that his future must begin in Ningpo. So he tried hard to find work there and even wanted to marry a girl in Ningpo. But all his efforts ended in vain. As Chinese tradition has it, anything a ghost said in dreams is always a riddle. No one can actually make a correct guess.

One day when Mrs. Wu went shopping, she met a woman, the wife of a friend to Mr. Wu. The friend had died early and the woman was left a small fortune, but fate was against her and she lost all the money in the stock market in Hong Kong, and had to return to Shanghai. She at least had a daughter here. Then she often came to see Mrs. Wu with the intention to borrow one or two yuan from her. She often came on the excuse that she had a girl to introduce to Genghua. After Genghua met the girl, she would come to say bad words about the girl in hopes that she could introduce another girl and borrow some more money. One day when she came again, Mrs. Wu asked her why she would introduce these girls to her son, since she knew they were bad. The woman had put herself in an awkward position. Anyway, she kept coming to introduce girls.

Once she came to say that she knew a girl who was very good-looking somewhat like Queen Elisabeth of England. She took Genghua to the girl's home, as she was familiar with her mother. The mother liked Genghua, but said nothing about Genghua and her daughter, because Genghua was jobless. She could not marry her daughter to a jobless person. And her daughter had work. She had another daughter, older than this one. She was married and worked in Canton. Her husband was the captain of a ship. She had a son and two daughters, all living with the grandma, whose husband had died. The grandma learned that Genghua's father was in Hong Kong. So she did not want to lose the contact and asked Genghua to come to her home to teach her grandson English. As Genghua had free time, he taught English for free. Only the mother would let Genghua stay for supper every time he came to teach. The girl, by the surname of Dong, came home after work for supper. So Genghua often met her. She *was* beautiful. When the woman came again, she told Mrs. Wu that the girl Dong had married a veteran and was divorced now. She meant that Genghua should not marry a divorced woman. Anyway, Genghua did not think of marrying her. Genghua taught the grandson for almost a year. The grandson would move to Canton to live with his mother. Genghua ceased teaching, but he kept in contact with the family. They were nice people.

Then the woman brought her daughter to the Wu family. She said that her daughter could also introduce girls to Genghua. Another day, the daughter took Genghua to an old man, Mr. Zhou, who was a cousin of Zhou Enlai, the premier of the State Council. He had been a lawyer before the Party came to power. Now he was on the payroll of the organization called the History Museum. Many older men of some social importance belonged to the History Museum and received a kind of pension from there. Although sometimes Genghua went to visit him and took him out to a restaurant, he never introduced any girl to Genghua. The old man also liked to write poems in the classical style, but his poems read like political slogans.

One day his friend Wei came, the son of their family doctor. But since the beginning of the Cultural Revolution, private doctors could not see patients anymore. And the red guards went to all the private doctors and took their valuables. The Party would not miss a family with some money. Wei came with a request that his father had a friend, who had a niece and needed someone to teach her English. The girl was applying to go to the US to see her aunt. Wei thought of Genghua and took Genghua to see his father's friend Mr. Jiang, also a doctor in a local clinic, but now he stayed at home owing to some disease. Mr. Jiang lived in a small room while the niece's family lived in a big room. Her mother was the sister of Mr. Jiang. The family had parents and two sons and two daughters. The niece was the elder daughter. The elder son worked in a factory and was learning how to draw Chinese paintings. The younger son had no job. Mr. Jiang insisted on paying Genghua, who had to receive the pay. It was the first time Genghua got paid for teaching English.

One day when the teaching was over Mr. Jiang told Genghua an anecdote about himself. When Shanghai was under occupation by the Japanese, he was unexpectedly arrested. He had done nothing wrong, even in the viewpoint of the Japanese. They did not beat him. In the end they let him go, apologizing and saying that they got the wrong person.

During this chaotic period, Genghua stayed at home most of the time. He read a lot of books, including Chinese history. One work contained the history of the twenty-four dynasties in China, in several volumes. He was very much interested in the character called Zhuge Liang in the Three Kingdoms period. The Chinese people deem Zhuge as the embodiment of wisdom. Liu Bei was an ambitious man and declared himself a relative of the emperor of the Han Dynasty, which developed into the Three Kingdoms period. Since Liu Bei gathered an army of his own, he had often escaped from the forces of other warlords, never won a battle, though he had two sworn brothers, who were brave and could fight. Someone suggested that he need a strategist as a counselor and recommended Zhuge to him. Zhuge was a hermit, but had a thorough knowledge of the situations all over the country. However, he was waiting for a suitable time to come out of his hut and surprise the nation. One day Liu Bei went to visit Zhuge with his sworn brothers. But when he knocked at the door, a servant came out to tell him that the master was not at home. So Liu Bei had to turn back. Another day when it was snowing, he thought that Zhuge might be at home. But to his disappointment, he was told that the master had gone to his friend's house. Next spring, he set his heart on seeing Zhuge this time. When he got there, he was told that the master was still asleep. He thought that it was not polite to wake the master, and so he waited outside the hut for hours. Then he heard that the master was chanting a poem:

> *Who will wake up first from the Dream?*
> *I myself know what my life is.*
> *I have enough of spring sleep in my hut;*
> *The sun outside windows comes up so belated.*

Then he said aloud, "Has some lowly person come to see me?" He was really trying the patience and temper of the visitors. But

Liu Bei did not get angry. He knew that a man of great talent was always eccentric. Then he was invited into the hut. As he was so polite and good-tempered, Zhuge began to like him. So he invited Liu Bei into his inner room, on the wall of which there hung a map drawn by hand. Zhuge pointed to the map and said to Liu, "Under the circumstances at present, the whole nation can be divided into three parts. Cao Cao has the strongest force and is now occupying the north of the Yangtze River. Sun Quan is now ruling the south of the Yangtze River. The western part of the nation in Shu Province is left for you to occupy. The present ruler there is a good-for-nothing." Liu agreed with his analysis. When Liu asked him to be his counselor, he accepted. People mentioned this event, saying that Zhuge knew the future division of three parts in the nation when he was still a hermit in his hut. It is just like a Chinese saying: a learned person knows all that happens under heaven though he never steps outside his house. The whole story was called "Three Visits to the Hut."

Mrs. Wu and Kunhua, the fourth son, often went to the reception room of the Xuhui police precinct to inquire about when their applications could be approved. When waiting in the line, they heard a funny conversation. A young applicant said that he had to go to Hong Kong since his father was seriously ill. The policewoman asked what use it would be for him to go, as he was not a doctor. The next time they went there again, they saw the young man there, too. When his turn came, he talked to the policewoman again. He told her that he had to go now since his father had died there. The policewoman said there was no use in going now, since his father was already dead.

Someone was vexed that Mrs. Wu and Kunhua often went there. So they used the same tricks. One evening, the new family in the second floor room complained that the Wu family upstairs made too much noise. Kunhua said that they were all adults and no children, how could there be too much noise. So a brawl broke out. Anyone who wants to have a brawl with anyone else can find any reason to start one easily. So both sides went to the police. The new family thought that any policeman there would be on their side, since they had been told to make the quarrel. But they did not know one fact: that the present policeman was not Comrade Yao, but Comrade Wu. Comrade Yao had made some mistakes and was now out of the position. Besides, Comrade Wu belonged to a group having different opinions in the Cultural Revolution from the group Comrade Yao was in. As a result, Comrade Wu did not support the new family. They had to return crestfallen.

Once two boys, playing in the lane, seeing the Wu brothers walking through the lane to the streets, came up to fight with them. Of course they were too young to actually fight with the brothers. The brothers knew that if they hit the boys and injured them, someone in the police precinct would use this as an excuse to criticize Wu family and use it as a reason to refuse their applications. However, they did not hit them. They wanted to catch them and bring them to the police and let the policemen there judge who were in the wrong. But at that time some neighbors came to say that the brothers should pardon them as they were still boys. The brothers could not say no to the neighbors, and the event ended peacefully.

One day Zhao, a classmate of Kunhua in the primary school, came to see him. He worked in the Foreign Trade Bureau of Shanghai and married a girl whose mother lived in Hong Kong. When he learned that Kunhua's father also lived in Hong Kong now, he came on a visit to refresh their old friendship. He had joined in the rebellious action and was now a member of a rebellious group, wearing a red arm band. He came just at the time when the Wu family was in the difficult situation to get their applications approved. Kunhua asked him if he knew anyone who could help solve their problem. Zhao introduced Kunhua, the fourth son, to Pan Guoping, the former commander-in-chief of the Shanghai Worker Revolutionary Rebellious Headquarters.

So Kunhua got to know Pan. Every time when Pan and his wife came to the Wu family, Kunhua would take them to the Red House, a Western-style restaurant, to have dinner. Pan's wife was a famous ballet dancer, Tan Yuanyuan, who was really beautiful. At that time under the instruction of the Party, all the things and money taken by the red guards were to be returned. Things, especially such things as gold, silver, and diamond, were forced to sell to the government banks at a very low price. A karat of diamond was only worth one hundred yuan of Chinese currency. If the communist government had not robbed those valuables from people, those people would have a lot of money nowadays as the prices of such valuable things rose very high.

CHAPTER 17 – THE WU FAMILY SEEKS HELP

According to the "price" on the "black market" helping people get permits or passports, one permit or passport would cost one thousand yuan at that time. Mrs. Wu thought that it was worth paying two thousand to get the permits as soon as possible. But Pan did not succeed in getting permits for them. He did not say anything about it. Simply, the applications were never approved. The conclusion was obvious: Pan could not get permits for them.

One day Pan arrived to visit the Wu family in a Jeep. This was a hint that the Wu family knew someone in power, because only people with some kind of power could ride in a Jeep. At that time no person could own a car of any kind. All the motor vehicles belonged to the government. Only officials of a certain rank could drive to work and back, or to attend to some political tasks. So this served as a hint to the neighborhood that the Wu family knew someone of a certain rank. From then on, the cadres in the neighborhood never made any trouble for the Wu family. They never knew that it was Pan.

A few months later, Kunhua got to know a man called Young Wang, who was married and had a little daughter. Supposedly, he was a relative of Wang Jinhai, though he did not say so. Wang Jinhai was a member of Shanghai Municipal Party Committee, a man of power. Pan had only a title, but no power. Young Wang often helped people solve problems, on condition, of course, that he would be paid. Mrs. Wu and Kunhua promised him two thousand yuan if he could get the permits for them. In such matters, there was no down payment. When the item sought was delivered into the hands of the requesters, the helper was paid. What if the requester got the thing and refused to pay? That would never happen, since the helper was a powerful person. But one day Young Wang came and confessed that someone in Xuhui police precinct refused his demand. He could not use the influence of Wang Jinhai anymore, because such things had to be done under the table. So the Wu family deduced that Pan had been turned down, too, though he did not confess it. Their applications seemed to be running aground.

Since the beginning of the Cultural Revolution, Genghua had been afraid to go to see those old gentlemen. Older men might have some kind of historical problems, which might affect him, or even his family, if he kept in touch with them. He did not go to see Secretary Zhang, as he knew that old cadres like him might have had some minor trouble and did not like people to bother them. He could only visit those who were sure to be without any political problems. Better just to stay home. So he began to read more books both in English and in classical Chinese.

The Chinese novel "Red Chamber Dream" is a great work of high literary value, world-renowned. Only it is a tragedy. Genghua was touched by it and read it more than once. The main female character Lin Daiyu, whose parents died early, lived with her grandma, who loved her very much. The main male character Jia Baoyu was her cousin. They grew up together and so their relationship was so close. They fell in love with each other when they came to know such things. Then another girl, also a cousin, Xue Baochai, came from Nanking to live with them, because her brother accidentally killed someone there. To avoid her son being put into prison, the mother, their father being dead early, took them both to the Jia family, since the men of this family were all courtiers. No one would dare to come to arrest anyone lodging in their residence. As the three cousins reached the age for marriage, the grandma wanted to choose a girl for her grandson Baoyu. She knew that her grandson loved the cousin Lin, not the cousin Xue, but Lin was frail of health and might not live long, while Xue was robust and seemed more likely to bear a healthy great grandson for her. Besides, Lin was quick-tempered and often quarreled with her grandson, though the grandson always gave in as he loved Lin so deeply. Xue was a tame, nice girl, kindly to everyone. Therefore, after she consulted her daughters-in-law, she made the decision to select the girl Xue as her granddaughter-in-law. To avoid trouble from her grandson, the decision was concealed from him. The girl Lin somehow found out and she purposely allowed her disease to progress by refusing to take her medicine. When the day came for the wedding, the grandson still did not know who was the bride. They had told him that he would marry Lin. So he went to the ceremony willingly. In accordance with tradition, the bride's head was covered with a red cloth throughout the ceremony. After the ceremony, the couple were sent to the bridal room, where the groom was to lift the red cloth from the face of his bride. When he did so, he was astounded to find that it was not his Lin, but the girl Xue. He ran out like a mad man to Lin's chamber in another building and found Lin dying in bed. He cried and cried. At last Lin was buried and he had to return to his bride. One night when he found that his wife was with child, he decided he had had enough. He became a monk in the end of the story.

The value of the novel does not just lie in the tragic plot, though it moves the readers. In the novel, there are many well-written poems. This is the literary value. The book also gives description in the life style of that time, the special dishes and how to cook them, and the author's opinion against the feudal ideas. There are also many jokes told and a few funny anecdotes. An anecdote goes like this: an old woman having a distant relationship with the Jia family came to visit the grandma one day. At dinner, she saw a boiled pigeon egg, she said, "How could a hen in a noble family lay such an exquisite egg so small?" To the laughter of all present. She was told that such an egg cost one tael of silver. When she used a pair of ivory chopsticks to pick a pigeon egg, it slipped from the ivory chopsticks onto the dirty floor and a maid standing aside picked it up and threw it away. The old woman sighed that a tael of silver was thus spent without even hearing a noise when the egg dropped on the floor. If a piece of silver fell on the floor, it might give a pleasing sound to the ear.

There are four great classical novels in Chinese: Three Kingdoms, The Beach, Journey to West, and Red Chamber Dream. The Beach describes the rebellion at the end of North Song Dynasty. As corruption was so severe among the government officials, people had no way to live peacefully and had to rise to arms. There were one hundred and eight persons, including three women, gathered on Mount Liang by a lake against the government. The novel is really a collection of individual stories about everyone of the one hundred and eight persons and how each of them turning from a civilian to be a rebel owing to the oppression of the officials. The first man who joined the rebels already on Mount Liang was Lin Chong, who was the head coach of the eight hundred thousand soldiers in the capital. He taught the soldiers how to use weapons in fighting. Official Tong was in charge of the army, his immediate boss. It was fine one spring day. Lin Chong took his wife to the suburb for the sightseeing. Coincidentally and unluckily, the son of the official Tong was also in the suburb. The son was a bad guy, always bullying common people. All of a sudden, he caught sight of the wife. She was so pretty. He liked pretty women. So he went up to flirt with her. The husband Lin Chong flared up and hit him on the chest. He did not know that the guy was the son of his boss. The son was about to tell his servants, who always followed him everywhere he went, to beat the husband, but a man beside him, by the mane of Lu, stopped him by whispering in his ear about who the husband was. Lin Chong was known as having the best kungfu in the capital. So the son had to go away and returned to his father's yamen where the family lived. But the image of the pretty woman always loomed in his mind's eye. He wanted the man Lu to think of a way to get the woman. Lu got an idea to set a trap for Lin Chong. If Lin was out of the way, they could even kidnap the woman from her home.

One day when Lin Chong walked in the street, he heard some-one shouting to sell a sword. Lin, as a man of kungfu, liked to collect swords. So he approached the seller and looked at the sword, a very good one. The seller said that he was in urgent need of money and sold it at a very low price. So Lin bought it and brought it home. A few days later, official Tong, his boss, sent Lu to him, saying that Tong learned that he bought a good sword and wanted to have a look at it. Lu told Lin to take the sword to his boss. Lin did not know it was a trick, and accordingly, took the sword to show to his boss. When he was waiting with the sword in the hand in the hall to be received by the boss, some of the Tong's bodyguards came to take him into their custody, accusing him of plotting to kill the boss as he had a sword in his hand. When he pleaded for himself no one would listen to him. So he was exiled to a remote place. His duty there was to take care of the haystacks which were used as fodder to the war horses. The man Lu followed him there. He wanted Lin Chong dead so that the son of the official Tong could possess his wife. Once Lin left the place to buy wine in a nearby town, Lu set fire to the haystacks. If it was found the neglect of Lin to have the haystacks burned, Lin would be put to death. In the middle of the process, Lin came back and saw the flame. Then he saw Lu was do-ing it, he was in deep wrath and went to kill Lu on the spot. Now he had to flee for his dear life. So he went to Mount Liang to join the rebels there. Meanwhile, his wife was taken by force to the yamen. But she killed herself by hanging as she knew that the son would certainly rape her. The stories of others were likewise pathetic.

The emperor sent troops after troops to conquer the rebels on Mount Liang, but all efforts were in vain. At last the emperor had to promise to give everyone of them official positions in the govern-ment. Most of them accepted the offer and a few rebuffed it and went away to hide somewhere as hermits. Many of those who ac-cepted the offer and got official positions were afterwards sent to fight another group of rebels and died in the battles.

One day when Genghua went to the home of his friend Zhang, he was told by his sister that Zhang was married and the couple were both approved to go to Hong Kong. Genghua expressed his congratulations. Then he learned that Miss Xu got married, too. The parents of her husband were in the US. That was what she wanted. She told Wei about it, when he went to see her and learned some information of her marriage. When she went to the street committee to ask for job, she met a young man there, who went there on the same purpose. It meant that they were both jobless. After their marriage, they both got jobs respectively. Xu was making a five-year plan, as she confessed to Wei, which sounded like the Party making five-year plans for the country. Her plan was to go to the US in five years. A great goal.

Ni had a girlfriend, Miss Zhang, whose father was in Canada. As the fathers of both sides were abroad, it seemed that the couple had the double relationship, a better condition. But it did not work any better for them at the time. They got married afterwards and had a daughter.

Liu had a girlfriend, too, Miss Wang, whose father was a scientist in Shanghai. But the scientist did not want his daughter to marry a man whose father was a reactionary, which would certainly affect his daughter and him politically. But the daughter persisted, and they did get married afterwards.

Ni and Liu separately brought their girlfriends to the Wu family. Both girls liked to talk with Mrs. Wu. Sometimes either of the girls would come for a chat with the mother even though Genghua was not at home. Supposing they were the girlfriends of Genghua's friends. Occasionally Miss Zhang would ask Mrs. Wu for a cigarette. She said that when she was feeling unhappy, she liked to smoke.

Genghua wanted to compile a Chinese–English Idiom Dictionary. He collected as many English idioms as possible, and then collected Chinese idioms. He matched them one by one if they were similar in meaning, such as "Kill two birds with one stone" and its Chinese equivalent is "Kill two vultures with an arrow." Or such as "There is no smoke without fire" and its Chinese equivalent, "There is no wave without wind." As there were so many idioms in both languages, it was an enormous undertaking. As later Genghua was assigned a job, he did not finish it. When he was introduced to Xie

Daren, a professor teaching Latin in Shanghai Second Medical University, who was compiling such a dictionary, he gave the data to him. When the idiom dictionary was published, the professor gave him a copy. Some of the idioms he had collected were used in it. At least, his efforts had not been a total waste.

Little Xue still came from time to time. His interest changed from practicing handwriting to learning fortune-telling. He got a book to tell fortunes. Kunhua liked that, too. So they discussed it whenever Little Xue came. The seventh sister of Xue family married a man, Mr. Chen, twelve years older than she, whose father lived in the US, too. Mr. Chen had work and lived in a big house. Then they had a baby boy. He was good-looking, very lovely, with skin that was semi-transparent, like the best-quality white jade. The eighth brother came to live with his sister to help look after the baby. Both the sister and the brother had no job. So they asked Genghua to teach the eighth brother English. Once or twice, the fourth son brought Pan there to play cards, as the sister and brothers, the eldest one, the sixth one and the eighth one, all had difficulties in their applications to go abroad. The fourth son of the Wu family brought Pan to them with the intention to help them for the problem.

One day, Little Xue brought a book called Back-Pushing Pictures, which is a book every dynasty forbade people to possess, nor to read. It was because the book had many pictures and some words underneath to imply which dynasty was the next. It said about the Qing Dynasty with these words: the hand showing hoof. In the Qing Dynasty, the official uniforms of courtiers had sleeves on their upper garments, the end of which was made like horse's hoofs. As to the Japanese invasion into China, it said something about a flag with a medical round piece in the center. The red round spot in the Japanese flag. When talking about the Communist Party, it said that those people wore a cap with eight corners. What the book implied could only be understood afterwards, not before. So Genghua checked the words of who would take over the leadership of the Communist Party, he could not make out the meaning and soon forgot it later.

The relationship between Chairman Mao and Vice Chairman Lin became worse because, according to the government document, Lin wanted to restore the position of the chairman of the country, but Mao did not agree. Liu Shaoqi had been the chairman of the country while Mao was the chairman of the Central Committee of the Party when Mao had been forced to retire to the background. After Liu was out of the picture, there was no more the position of the chairman of the country. Mao said that Lin wanted to be the chairman to share power with him. But the reasoning was so poor. Lin was at that time the vice chairman of the Party, the official successor to Mao when Mao died. Why should he want to be the chairman of the country? He could just wait for Mao's death. So easy and no risk. It was very probably that Mao wanted his wife Jiang Qing to be his successor. So he intended to find an excuse to down Lin Biao, like he had downed Liu, to clear the way for his wife. The conclusion was very much correct that after the death of Lin Biao, he planned to get rid of Zhou, the premier.

On the 13th of September, 1971, the Party told all nation that an event happened that Lin, his wife and his son died in a plane crashed in Mongolian Republic. How could a leader's plane so easily crash? The explanation was not so satisfactory. Then a rumor was in circulation that the plane was downed by a missile from the inner Mongolian area. The commander of the army stationed there was General You Taizhong at that time. In Communist China, rumors are always based on facts, as facts are always covered up. The saying "Rumors have short legs" is not fit to use in Communist China. Facts have to be circulated in the form of a rumor. Or the Party declares the fact as a rumor as they cannot deny the fact some other way. I invent a new idiom that rumor ends in transparency. If the facts are shown in a glass house for everyone to see, who will make up a rumor and circulate it? The Party explained that Lin's son plotted to kill Mao using antiaircraft guns to level at the train Mao rode in from Hangzhou to Beijing. But Mao used a false move and safely arrived in Beijing. When their plot failed, they wanted to escape to Russia. The party gave their truth to the Chinese people, and to the world, too.

Many years later, Zhang Ning, the girlfriend of Lin's son, wrote a book narrating the event. She was with Lin family when the event took place. According to her, readers can draw such a conclusion that Lin's death was a trap set up by Mao and Zhou Enlai, the premier. Mao had talks with some concerned leaders of local governments and warned them to keep it a top secret, but he let someone leak it to Lin's wife and son, as Lin was sick in bed. The secret leaking out was made to sound like Mao wanted to have Lin arrested or even killed. Lin's wife and son fell in panic and wanted to escape. They dragged Lin out of the house and pushed him into the car. The chief guard Li, who was sent here by Zhou Enlai to guard Lin for his safety, got into the car first so that Lin's family members would naturally follow him in. But when Lin family sat in the car, he jumped out. He shot at himself at his left arm so that he would be sent to a clinic for treatment. If he went with Lin family, he would die in the crash, too. He had to have known the result and acted like that to shun the inevitable death. When Lin's car sped away, the soldiers could easily stop it, but no one took any action. Lin family got to the military airport and climbed on the plane especially used for them. A few minutes after the plane rose into the air, it seemed that the plane wanted to re-land, but all lights in the airport were out and the runway was in dark. How could that happen? It seemed that all this was arranged beforehand. They had to fly north. The Party added that at first Lin wanted to fly to Canton to establish another government against Mao, but as there was not enough gas in the tank of the plane, he had to fly to Russia, taking the shortest route. As the plane was crossing the borderline, it was shot down and fell in the territory of Mongolian Republic. Although Chinese people had doubts about the whole thing, yet they did not care that Lin died. He supported Mao, or the Cultural Revolution would not have happened. There is a Chinese saying that "when there are no more rabbits, even stray dogs will be cooked." This was typical of Lin's sayings. It was said that Mao wanted to wipe out all the old cadres from the Long March and YanAn to make way for the Gang of Four, Jiang Qing, his wife, Wang Hongwen, the vice chairman of the party at that time, Zhang Chunqiao and Yao Wenyuan. Later,

Mao decided to wipe out Zhou Enlai as well. His intention was as clear as the nose on his face.

On the 29th of September, 1972, China and Japan established diplomatic relations. China declared it would give up its demand for war indemnity from Japan. Why was China so generous? Mao said once that the Chinese Communist Party should thank Japan for invading China. Why? Because if Japan had not invaded China, the Communist Party would have been wiped out long before by the army of Chiang Kai-shek, which was much the stronger one. But with the invasion, Chiang Kai-shek had to maneuver most of his troops against Japan. The Communist Party escaped destruction. It was a life and death opportunity Japan had provided for them.

Chapter 18 – Genghua Starts To Translate Classics & Cultural Revolution Ends

All these political events seemed to have nothing to do with Genghua. He buried his head in books, reading and writing. He began to translate Chinese classical poems into English. Formerly, Chinese men of letters had translated them into English in a modern style without meter and rhyme. Genghua sought to transpose the Chinese classical styles at least into English meter and rhyme so as to reflect the sense of the original. The one he first tried was *Plum Blossoms* by Wang Anshi of Song Dynasty:

> *At a wall corner some plum trees grow;*
> *Alone against cold white blossoms blow.*
> *Aloof one knows they aren't the snow,*
> *As faint through air soft fragrances flow.*

This version was later published in an English magazine in China after the Cultural Revolution.

A famous essay was composed by Liu Yuxi (772–842 AD) of the Tang Dynasty with the title "Eulogy on My Humble Abode":

Known will hills be if fairies dwell, no matter high or low; and charmed will waters be if dragons lurk, no matter deep or shallow.

A humble abode though this is, my virtues make it smell sweet. Verdant are the stone steps overgrown with moss, and green seems the screen as the grass seen through it. I chat and laugh only with great scholars and have no intercourse with the ignorant. I can play zither and read my sutras; no unpleasant music to grate on my ears and no red-tape to weary my mortal form. Zhuge's residence in Nanyang and Ziyun's inhabitance in Xishu are both like what Confucius quoth, "How can it be humble?"

Zhuge was mentioned before; he lived as a hermit in a hut in Nanyang, and Liu Bei went to see him three times. Yang Ziyun (53–18 BC) was a philosopher and writer in West Han Dynasty, leading a simple life. Therefore, the writer of this essay said that since the two famous people lived simply, no one should say that their housing was humble just like his own.

One day, Genghua met his fat friend, who was chanting something, counting on a long key chain. Generally a Buddhist believer, when chanting some Buddhist sutra, or just Amitabha Buddha, will count the rosary of beads. But in the years of the Cultural Revolution, it was deemed superstitious and would be criticized. The fat friend told Genghua that as he could not use a rosary of beads, he used a key chain instead, and as he could not chant Amitabha Buddha, he now chanted "Long Live Chairman Mao." He explained that the purpose of chanting Amitabha Buddha was to make one calm, which would help him keep fit. As long as he could meet his goal, why could he not just chant "Long Live Chairman Mao" instead? If anyone heard him chanting this, no one could criticize him. How funny.

From time to time, Genghua went to see the Zhu family. To his surprise, the daughter had married to a man, whose family lived in Cambodia. Later, the husband went to Hong Kong and his wife, the daughter of Zhu family, went with him. At that time, their grandma died. The mother asked Genghua if he knew anyone who wanted to buy their house at the price of 30,000 US dollars, because they would soon go to Hong Kong, too, and needed foreign currency. Genghua was sorry to say that he did not know anyone who wanted to buy a house. But he congratulated them.

One day a friend came and brought a book describing some terrible events happened in some central provinces of China. During the fighting period, in a small town, a male schoolmaster was killed in the fight. Some people in the neighborhood came to cut his flesh or organs from his body to take home and cook them for eating. There is a belief among illiterate people that what organ you eat will benefit your health in that part of your body. So the book described that someone cut the kidneys of the schoolmaster and someone even cut off his genital.

Mrs. Wu and Kunhua thought of a strategy for their application. Since the Xuhui police precinct would not approve their application, why wouldn't they move to other precincts? This had to be done through housing exchange and the approval of the housing department. Anyway, they could at least look for some housing they wanted to move to. So Genghua wrote housing exchange information on paper for them and the brothers went to stick them one by one on walls and lamp posts. They did not want people to come directly to their home to have a look. So they put the address of their cousin on the paper, explaining that the housing of the address was not for exchange. Anyone, who wanted to see the housing for exchange, had to write to that address and leave a contact method. If one had work, he would use the phone number of his work place as contact means.

Many people in Shanghai wanted to exchange housing. Mostly they wanted to change the environment. The quickest way was direct contact. So groups of people gathered on some streets without much traffic. Genghua and his brother went to different places with such activities. Sometimes they would bring home a stranger to look at their rooms. Other times they would go to other's house to look at theirs. But all was without result.

The Wu family wanted to move into Luwan District because the fourth son had a classmate, Zhao, working in the Foreign Trade Bureau, who knew someone in that police precinct. Maybe that would help Mrs. Wu and the fourth son to get their applications approved. But it would limit their chances at the housing exchange. Then the auntie came to visit them in Shanghai and suggested that she knew someone in Suzhou who might be able to help. But if it didn't work out they would not be able to move back to Shanghai. Moving at that time in China was very difficult. It required police approval from both cities. So they finally decided not to take the chance.

One day Genghua went to the housing exchange and got to know an old lady, Ms. Tan, who was a pianist in Shanghai Conservatory of Music. Her brother was a famous violinist in China, Tan Shuzhen. Her sole son, Li Mingduo, was also a highly regarded pianist. The father-in-law of the son had also been in dye business and Genghua knew his name. Small world. So they got closer and Mrs. Wu invited mother and son (and his wife) for home supper. Ms. Tan even introduced Genghua to a pretty girl, her private pupil, but of course the girl's mother thought him unsuitable since he was unemployed.

On the 18th of January, 1974, another movement was under way, called "Criticize Lin (Biao), Criticize Confucius." Then some words were added exhorting the people to "Criticize Zhou," that is Zhou Enlai, the premier. Mao wanted to get Zhou out of the way. But this was not easy, as all the old generals and cadres backed Zhou. The Gang of Four could not stand the fact that the army was not under their control, though even there they had some support. Just not enough.

On the 1st of June, 1974, Zhou Enlai was seriously ill and was sent to the hospital. He was suffering from cancer. He stayed in hospital till the 8th of January, 1976, when he died at the age of seventy-six. Many Chinese wept for him. It was not so much that they liked him, but that they hated Mao and the Gang of Four. So they showed they liked Zhou, the political enemy of Mao and the Gang of Four. Similarly, after the slaughter on TianAnMen Square, people suddenly began to praise Mao, by which they meant to criticize Deng, at whose order the slaughter was carried out. This was the only means by which the Chinese people could "vote."

Mao was ill, too, at that time. On the 28th of July, 1976, a severe earthquake hit Tangshan Town. The casualties were officially reported 240,000. But the estimate was at least 300,000. Superstitious people said that it was a sign that an important event would happen.

On the 9th of September, Mao died. The Party decided that people of the whole country should gather together to mourn the death of Mao. The people may have come together, but they were glad in their hearts, not mournful. They hoped that change would happen and things would turn for the better.

On the 6th of October, the Gang of Four were arrested. This signaled the end of the Cultural Revolution. But the judgment of them in the court was really a ridiculous political drama played publicly. The speech Jiang Qing made in the court sounded like a composition of the child. What would happen to China if the Gang of Four ruled the country? A ridiculous thing was said by a grandson of Mao, which appeared on the Internet; "My grandfather (Mao) started the Cultural Revolution with the intention to fight against the Gang of Four." The head of the Gang of Four was Jiang Qing, the wife of Mao, the grandmother of the speaker, who meant that his grandfather wanted to fight his grandmother publicly. Why wouldn't they just fight each other in their bedroom? People would ask.

Then people pinned their hope on Deng as he was the famous one "insisting on going the capitalist road" as Mao had criticized him. Deng also said that he wanted to let part of the Chinese people get rich first. Chinese people hated socialism and welcomed capitalism. But later, to their great disappointment, they got capitalism only economically, but still the socialism politically. Even the capitalism economically belonged not to them, but actually to the children and relatives of the Party leaders. They were the part of the Chinese people Deng actually meant.

An exact example of Deng's policy was that an ordinary man made a fortune by selling cooked sunflower seeds with delicious taste. Before long, he was poor again because the government fined him penniless on account of tax-dodging. Communist government can always say that this one is guilty of this and that one is guilty of that. Who can say otherwise? They don't need to produce convincing evidence, or only need to give false evidence.

Why did China go the capitalist road economically, but insist on going the socialist road politically? Deng Xiaoping had a specious theory about it, which was that China was now on the initial stage of socialism. According to the basic theory of communism using which the Party educated people at the beginning of their reign, communism is the last and highest stage of society system, higher than the capitalism. Communism itself can be divided into two substages: socialism is the first and lower substage while communism is the last and higher substage. That means that even socialism is the higher stage than the capitalism in the society system since it is included in the communism, the lower substage of communism. Now as China is on the initial stage of socialism, it is still on the stage higher than the capitalism, how can China develop to the lower stage of capitalism, even economically? The correct saying should be that China is not advancing, but retreating to the lower stage of capitalism. Does it mean that Deng bring China from a forward position to a backward position? From Mao to Deng, they always have strange theories to fool people. The Communist Party always commands people what to do under the ear-pleasing cloak of weird theory.

Chapter 19 – Genghua Finds Official Work Teaching English

After the Cultural Revolution, Genghua's destiny turned for the better. It really began with the presentation of credentials of the first ambassador of West Germany in China, because Bai, Genghua's classmate, was the interpreter for West Germany on the occasion. He was sent to work in German embassy as the first secretary and often had a chance to see Chinese leaders and their assistants. Generally secretaries in embassies are considered to be international spies. As Genghua still kept up correspondence with Bai, the police in Shanghai thought that Bai might be using Genghua for some espionage plans. They sent two persons, a man, Comrade Luo, and a woman, Comrade Jin, to see Genghua and wanted him to report to them if Bai asked him to do anything illegal, against China's interests. Genghua promised that he would do so without doubt. But as a matter of fact, Genghua knew Bai was not the type to get involved in any such thing, and in the end, Genghua learned from Bai that as Germany needed someone as an interpreter in the embassy in China, and a relative of Bai's mother working in German government recommended Bai for the interpreter position, and that is how Bai got the appointment.

Genghua was still jobless, and the police decided that it would not look good for China if Bai came to Shanghai and met the jobless Genghua. Of course, Genghua had never told Bai in his letters to him that he was jobless. The authorities instructed the Street Committee to give Genghua a job. It was summer. The first job Genghua got was to sell watermelon and fruits in a store as a temporary, not a permanent shop assistant. Now Genghua was happy. It was the first job, though temporary, he had ever got after twenty years of being jobless. He had income and was in a high spirits. He often joked with fellow workers and customers while selling fruit.

After summer, Genghua was sent to work in a food factory to make moon cakes. It would soon be the Mid-Autumn Festival. Moon cakes would be on the market. What he did was that he took up one flour ball, which was ready, and pressed it flat, then put some stuffing, which was also ready, on the flour and wrapped the stuffing with the flour. Then he put the whole thing into a mold and when he took it out of the mold, he put it on an iron tray, which would go into an oven to bake. Once he witnessed that a fellow worker picked up a ball of stuffing from the dirty ground he carelessly let it fall and stuffed it directly into the flour ball. In Genghua's opinion, the stuffing should be thrown away. From then on, Genghua never ate any moon cakes.

When the Mid-Autumn Festival was over, Genghua was assigned a job in a candy factory. Spring Festival would come and candy was in demand in great quantities. Any piece of candy, once it fell on the dirty ground, was just thrown away. Sometimes a worker, if he was hungry enough, would put a piece of candy into mouth. That was no problem.

The candy-making process was like that: sugar was put into a big pot for melting. The melted sugar was poured onto a stainless steel surface with cold water running beneath it to cool. A little hardened material was sent into a machine to cut into small pieces of general candy size. Then the pieces were conveyed into another machine to be wrapped in colored paper, ready for sale.

After Spring Festival, he went to work in a printing and dye-ing mill. He worked two shifts at a baling press. He had lunch in the factory canteen. He met Ni there. Ni worked there already for a few years. Since Ni got work, Genghua had not seen him lately. He got married and still lived with his mother. The couple slept in the attic. It was really something tough for the bride. She was a nice woman. Their applications were refused many times. But a few years later the couple got passports to go to Canada through *her* fa-ther's influence with Liao Chengzhi, who was in charge of the office of the central government dealing with oversea Chinese. The office was directly under the State Council. Liao Chengzhi was the son of Liao Zhongkai, who was a comrade of Sun Yat-sen in the revolution against the Qing Dynasty, the last feudal dynasty in China.

Then Genghua was sent to Shanghai Fifty-Ninth Middle School to teach Physics as a substitute for a woman teacher in her mater-nity leave. In fact, he almost forgot physics he had learned in senior middle school, though the class he was to teach was that of the ju-nior school. He wrote down what he would teach with the aid of other teachers. If students wanted to ask questions more than what he was prepared, he would be in an awkward situation. Luckily, the students in that class never asked questions. At that time in middle schools, many students did not want to study. Therefore, students were divided into different classes. Those students who wanted to study were put into the same class. Those who did not want to study were in other classes. Genghua taught the class no one wanted to study.

Through the influence of the police, the school let Genghua keep working there, though the physics teaching task was over. Generally a substitute teacher would be dismissed when the one he worked for was back. The school authorities decided that Geng-hua would teach English in fall semester after summer vacation. He worked as a temporary. Now Genghua felt like a fish to be put back in water. There was another temporary teacher of English, who had graduated from Shanghai Foreign Languages Institute. A few days after the beginning of school, Genghua and the man was told to take a test of English with all the temporary teachers of English from other middle schools. When the result of the test came, the authorities found that the mark of Genghua was higher than that of the man graduated from the institute. So other teachers of English always came to ask questions when they had some difficulties in their teaching. Many teachers of English in this school did not have diplomas from any colleges.

Teachers of every subject formed a teaching group. The leading teacher of English group liked Genghua and always discussed teaching problems with him. The nickname of this teacher was Ahgou, meaning a dog. There were several classes of the third grade in senior middle school, equivalent to the twelfth grade. Students would graduate after a year. Ahgou was in charge of the first class and also taught English to it. Genghua taught four classes. Students in the second and third classes were good students, who wanted to enter universities. Students in the fourth and fifth classes did not want to have higher education. They just wanted to graduate and be given a job. So it was easy for Genghua to teach in the second and third classes. Once he read aloud a story from the text book with high and low tones alternately. When he finished, the class applauded their appreciation. Generally Chinese teachers of English read English like they were reading Chinese, without rhythm.

The difficulty with the fourth and fifth classes for Genghua was not in teaching, but in maintaining the discipline. Genghua was not a person to keep discipline in a class. Only when the teacher in charge of the class stood outside the classroom and watched through the window did the students get quiet and let Genghua continue teaching. Otherwise, Genghua just taught what he had prepared in the noise of the class.

But another good chance befell Genghua. As the government wanted to develop higher education, many university authorities were instructed to establish an affiliated college under the university. The second son of Mr. Wu, Genghua's step-brother, knew someone in Shanghai Science & Technology University and asked him to recommend Genghua to University authorities, who planned to have two departments for English course in the newly established affiliated college, a teaching department and a translation department. The teaching department would get students. So through recommendation they employed many people. Then a test was held for all of them. Genghua's mark was in 90's, very high among the testees. Genghua was assigned to teach English in the teaching department. So Genghua quit the job in the middle school and began to work in the affiliated college of the Shanghai Science & Technology University. The teachers in the middle school envied Genghua and congratulated him for being able to teach in a college without even a diploma from one.

A Mr. Cai was one of English teachers. He had graduated from Shanghai Foreign Languages Institute. He was allotted a job in a small town and did not go there. So he became jobless. In his condition, he was not a social youth. He married a jobless woman and had a son. Four English teachers came from the original university and one of them was the leader of the English teaching group. He was Mr. Lu. As a rule university teachers had no need to stay in the office the whole day. They had to come when there were classes. And when there were no classes, they did not need to come. But Mr. Lu decided that every teacher should come every day and sit in the office even if there were no classes that day. So Cai and Genghua did not like it.

Then Cai and Genghua found another problem. All those recently hired got the permanent positions except Cai and Genghua. If they considered that Genghua had never been in any university and gave him only a temporary position, it was understandable. But Cai was a college graduate. It was unfair not to give him a permanent position. No one knew how such things worked. On what basis the authorities decided who would be the permanent and who would be the temporary?

Genghua explained all the texts in detail, emphasizing all the basic grammar the students should learn. He gave lectures about literature and made a list of rules governing how English words should be pronounced, both of which were welcomed by students. But all this made Mr. Lu look incompetent by comparison. In China (and not only in China), a leader prefers to be seen as superior in all respects to anyone under his leadership.

Cai and Genghua were not happy working as temporaries while all others were permanent. Another opportunity came in 1977. East China Normal University in Shanghai was then in great need of translators and teachers of various languages, including English language. They put an ad in newspapers. The applicants had to pass a test. Cai read the ad and told Genghua. They talked openly in the office about it. So all the faculties knew it. The authorities of the college did not like the idea that Cai and Genghua went to take the test, but since Cai and Genghua did not really the formal or permanent employees, they had the right to go anywhere they liked.

So Cai and Genghua went for the test. They both were accepted as temporary teachers. Genghua scored highest on the written test. His grade on the oral test was not so good as he did not have much practice speaking English. When East China Normal University handed in paper work to the high education bureau of Shanghai, which managed things for universities and colleges, to demand that all the recent employees were approved to be permanent, the result was that all but Cai and Genghua were granted. This was because the authorities in the Shanghai Science & Technology University knew someone in the high education bureau and complained that East China Normal University had induced two of their best teachers to work there. So the bureau refused to give permanent positions to Cai and Genghua. But it was better to teach as temporaries in East China Normal University than in the Science & Technology Affiliated College, as the former was an old important university while the latter was only a new small affiliated college.

Cai taught English in the university's night school. At first Genghua taught English in the Chinese Language Department. The students in that class learned Chinese language, but they still needed to be taught English. There was a special class managed by the night school. The purpose of this class was to train the teachers, including lecturers and associate professors, of this university in taking TOEFL and GRE tests, so they could go to the US for further studies in their research fields. A special office was set up. There were different classes for students to learn grammar, fast reading of texts, and to train the listening ability.

Suddenly the grammar teacher, Mr. Ye, fell seriously ill and could no longer give lessons. So the vice director of the training office, Mr. Hu, was in urgent need of another teacher strong in grammar to fill the position. He thought of Genghua, as he had done best on the test. So Genghua was transferred to that office, teaching grammar. The director of the training office was Mr. Chi, who was a Party member. A Party member could always be appointed to the position of a leader. That is why many people want to join the Communist Party—the path to officialdom and to power. Mr. Chi was right now intent on some procedures to go to the US and left all the duties of the office in the hands of Mr. Hu with the assistance of a woman taking all the office chores. Mr. Hu himself took care of teaching arrangements.

Later Mr. Hu learned that Genghua's father was in Hong Kong and asked if he could get him a foreign-made calculator. To keep his teaching job, Genghua had to promise and wrote to his father. A few weeks later, Genghua got the calculator and gave it to Mr. Hu, who was happy and treated Genghua more kindly.

After a few weeks, Genghua was struck with a wonderful idea. He suggested that as students had to take TOEFL as the last goal of this training, why did the teacher not just give them some tests like TOEFL? Genghua offered to prepare a test paper just in the form of TOEFL. Mr. Hu thought it was a very good idea and supported Genghua. But Genghua had no idea what TOEFL paper looked like. So Mr. Hu found one from a student who had taken the test. The TOEFL taker was allowed to keep the test paper after the test. Mr. Hu gave it to Genghua. Therefore, following the form of the TOEFL paper, Genghua created one of his own. For the listening part, Genghua wrote the questions and answers, and Mr. Hu asked an American teacher to read it into a tape, and the time elapsed was strictly kept to the original. Then he designed three test papers after the TOEFL, enough for the semester. The next semester, there would be new students and he could use the same paper over again.

Genghua had classes for two afternoons a week. He spent four hours for one afternoon. On other days he could stay at home and did whatever he liked. For classes, he first taught grammar needed in TOEFL. After the grammar book finished, he gave students test paper of his own that he had created. He gave the test just in a manner like the formal TOEFL test, the same time limit, from the listening part to the reading part. After the test and a recess, he discussed with the students how to solve the questions. He went question by question. In the listening part, as the listening ability of Chinese students was poor, he told the students some testing skills. First they should not listen to the passage before the questions as it was all the same. Using this time, they had to read the answers below to get some ideas. Then he requested them to grasp some key words in the question when listening to the tape, and with these, to quickly decide the answer.

For the second part, the grammar questions, he instructed the students how to analyze the sentence structures of every question, by which means most mistakes in the sentence could be found. For example, if the question word in the sentence was an adjective, but through structure analysis, the student found that the word there was an adverb, that's where the mistake was.

For the reading part, the student could skip the reading passage and go directly to the question. There must be a key word or key words in the question. Using this or these, the student would go to the beginning of the passage for the first question and could find the answer there. The answer to the last question was always in the end of the passage. These were testing skills he invented.

Chapter 20 – Bai Helps with Travel Permits

Comrade Luo and Comrade Jin from the police station would ask Genghua to meet them once in a while. Genghua told them about his father's condition, living in Hong Kong alone and sick. They promised to help with it. But next time, after a few months, when they met again, they did not mention anything about it. From experience, Genghua could tell that their help also ended in no result. Then they offered to help Genghua to get a permanent position in the university he was working. If this could be resolved, at least Genghua would have a feeling of settling down. However, no result turned up. Genghua was still a temporary. Once Cai and Genghua went to the high education bureau in Shanghai to argue with the cadres there that since the policy of the Party was to select one according to the test marks from the highest down. Since Genghua was the first in the test, why was he denied the permanent position while some whose marks were not so high were approved to be permanent? But the cadres there just stared at him and made no answer. It seemed as if they were saying what you could do to us if we denied you the permanent position. Genghua could do nothing to them. They had the power to decide things. Genghua did not have it.

As to Cai, who taught in this university, he had quit the job there after some time. The policy of Deng permitted people to go the capitalist road. So Cai and his wife started to be self-employed by buying and selling clothes, especially coats and trousers of jeans. Thus, their income was much more than the salary Cai got from the university. So Cai and Genghua seldom met. Unexpectedly, one day, when Genghua was walking in the campus, he saw the elder brother of Chen family, who had passed the test and worked as a translator now. His younger brother took the test, too, but failed. And another day, he met another friend, Pang, who also worked here as a translator. He knew three foreign languages: English, Italian, and Japanese. He was a nephew of Prof. Qian Zhongshu, famous in China, who was one of the translators rendering books of Mao into English. Qian had written a letter about him to Wu Zhaohua, another nephew, who killed himself during the Cultural Revolution. Wu Zhaohua had been a pupil of Mr. Wang and Genghua met him when they all gathered in the park. Wu's father had been the mayor of Shanghai in KMD government. Two sentences in Qian's letter read as: He (Pang) looks like dry wood. Dry wood easily catches fire. Very funny description. When Genghua and Pang were both social youths, jobless, Genghua often went to see Pang and played Chinese chess with him. Pang read Chinese classics and memorized 700 or 800 Chinese classical poems. Whenever they were playing chess, Pang would recite poem after poem in a very low voice that Genghua could not make out.

Genghua received a letter from Bai. He no longer worked as the first secretary in the German embassy. He worked now for a German company as their sales representative in China and invited Genghua to Beijing to renew the old friendship as they had separated for so long. Bai and Genghua had not seen each other for more than twenty years. Since Genghua had classes only for two afternoons, he took one afternoon off and went to Beijing for five days. He went by train. At that time common people could not afford to travel by air. When Genghua arrived at the railway station in Beijing, Bai came to meet him in a taxi. They went to the hotel Bai stayed in. The room had two beds. They had a long talk about all the things concerning both after the long parting. So Genghua seized the opportunity to ask a favor of his friend. Genghua wanted Bai to hand in a letter about his father living alone and sick in Hong Kong and the applications of his mother and brother could not be approved for more than ten years. If such a letter could reach the hand of any of the national leaders, the problem would soon be solved. So Bai wrote a letter to a Chinese high-ranked official he knew personally, enclosing Genghua's petition letter, and asking him to hand the letter to Yu Qiuli, a vice premier of the State Council at that time.

Next day was Friday and Bai still needed to work for a few hours. Genghua went alone to visit the Palace Museum, known to foreigners as the Forbidden City. Many treasures were stored there on display. Besides artifacts of gold and silver, there were all sorts of gems, such as ruby, sapphire, amber, emerald, etc., all the chinaware made in previous dynasties, all the paintings drawn by the ancients, and other treasures. The throne for the emperor was there, too, for visitors to see, but not allowed for anyone to sit on. If a visitor could be permitted to sit on for a little while only for the payment of money, the museum could make a great fortune in the years. But the throne would soon be worn out. When Genghua returned to the hotel, Bai was already back from office. They had supper in the restaurant on the ground floor.

On Saturday, they went to the Great Wall in a taxi. Most of it collapsed and the part travelers could climb on was repaired. The Great Wall had been built for defense against the invaders from north, but the Mongolians from north and the Qing clan from north both crossed the Great Wall and ruled China. What was the use of the Great Wall? Some ancient people said that if a ruler could not treat his people well and let them have enough to eat, his dynasty would sooner or later crumble, all the same result with or without the Great Wall.

On Sunday, Bai took Genghua to visit the Temple of Heaven, where the emperors went to worship Heaven for its blessing. It was constructed in 1420, in the eighteenth year of the reign of Emperor

Yongle of Ming Dynasty. There was an echo wall that was circular. If one stands in the center and speak in normal voice, he can hear the echo of his voice louder than his original one. But it does not affect people around him. A miracle of architectural technology.

Genghua left Beijing on Monday, because he would have classes on Tuesday. Bai sent him to the railway station in a taxi. Genghua rode in the train back to Shanghai, harboring the hope that applications of his mother and brother would soon be granted. Who could resist the instruction of a vice premier? In a few weeks, they did get their permanent permits to go to Hong Kong.

Just before they were about to leave Shanghai, Mr. Wu came back from Hong Kong. Since his wife and son had not gone to Hong Kong, he came to see what the matter was. Then Mr. Wu decided that his wife and the fourth son had better leave for Hong Kong right away, separately from himself. He wanted to stay a little longer to see some old friends in Shanghai. This would surely be his last visit to Shanghai, as he was now round eighty. So Mrs. Wu and her son went all by themselves. Ahmei, their former maidservant, was asked to come and stay for a while to look after Mr. Wu, and Mr. Wu's second son came to see him together with his wife and two children. Mr. Wu liked his granddaughter and grandson. He paid in Hong Kong for a television of foreign make so that the second son could pick it up in Shanghai. Mr. Wu told the second son to give his old set to Genghua. .

As usual, Genghua went to classes. One day in the street near his home, he met the mother of Dong family, her beautiful daughter looking like Queen Elisabeth II. Mrs. Dong came to see Genghua. She learned that Genghua's mother and brother had left for Hong Kong. And now Genghua had a job. She hinted that perhaps Genghua and her daughter could be suitable together. But the daughter was almost his age, and Genghua had to say that he would prefer to marry a girl much younger so that it would be easier to give birth to a child. He was himself a little over forty now.

To Genghua's surprise, his female cousin, Youfeng, came to see Mr. Wu one evening. She was the niece of Mr. Wu's first wife, who had died some time after the death of Genghua's grandma. She intended to introduce a girl to Genghua. The girl's name was Cheng Beili. They met in Youfeng's home. The girl was pretty, born in the year of the ox, like Genghua, and was twelve years younger. Someone superstitious would say that two oxen would fight. They were not suitable to each other. But at first sight, Genghua had an intuition that the girl was his destined wife. After half an hour's talk, the girl wanted to go home early. So the matchmaker told Genghua to see the girl home for safety's sake.

The matchmaker had lied to the girl about Genghua's age. She had made it sound like Genghua was only six years older than the girl. But Genghua did not know at that time. When the girl reached home safe and sound, and Genghua said goodbye, having made a date for another meeting on West Nanking Road, close to her home.

The appointment was at six in the evening of the next day. Genghua liked to arrive a bit early and the girl was, of course, not there yet. Genghua waited and waited, but the girl never made her appearance. Almost one hour elapsed and the girl was nowhere to be seen. Genghua thought that perhaps she would not come. So he decided that he would wait till seven o'clock. If the girl still did not appear, it meant that they were not destined to be together. At seven o'clock sharp on Genghua's wrist watch, just as Genghua was about to leave, there the girl came, out of the neon lights from the shop windows. Genghua was happy and thought that his intuition was right. The girl apologized and Genghua did not care as long as she was here. They went to a restaurant for supper. Then the girl asked Genghua his age, and Genghua answered truthfully. So the girl told him that the matchmaker had lied to her. Genghua was sorry. Anyway, they got on well. The girl thought that Genghua was at least an honest man, though he was much older than she. The girl had already rejected a boy only six years older than she.

Genghua invited her to come to his home on the coming Sunday so that she could meet his father. She came and stayed for supper. Genghua's father liked the girl. For next few days, some friends of Mr. Wu came to see him. Even Mr. Hu, Genghua's university colleague, came to see his father. When Mr. Hu mentioned a friend of his father's, it turned out to be a friend of Mr. Wu's, too. By Chinese tradition, their relationship got closer. Mr. Hu's father came from Ningpo, too, but his parents were now both dead. Later, when Genghua's career developed with the aid of Mr. Hu, he came to understand what his grandma had told him in his dream. It was that his future depended on a person of Ningpo origin, not that he had to go to Ningpo. In Chinese belief, a ghost knows the future, but he or she never says it directly. In due time what he or she says will come true.

On Friday, Mr. Wu would return to Hong Kong. The second son bought ticket for him. A relative came that day. He would accompany Mr. Wu to Canton together with Genghua. The second son would see his father to the train station of Shanghai. Genghua and the relative went with Mr. Wu. In Canton, they bought another ticket for Mr. Wu and saw him off by train to Hong Kong. Mrs. Wu and the son would meet him there.

Now Genghua and the relative had all the weekend to themselves. So they toured in the city and to some spots of renown in the suburbs. They went to Yuexiu Park, named after Yuexiu Hill. The hill became widely known because Zhao Tuo, the prince of Yue, had built Zhaohan Terrace on the hill in West Han Dynasty. They also went to see Whampoa Military Academy, which, it was said, was one of the four famous military academies in the world. The other three are West Point in the US, Imperial Japanese Army Academy in Japan, and Royal Military Academy Sandhurst in England. They went to a restaurant popular in Canton. They did not order dishes with meat of snake or rat, much less the brain of monkey. It was very cruel for people in Canton to eat the brain of monkey. It is said that when a customer orders the brain of monkey, a pot with fire underneath is served first, put in the middle of the table. Then a waiter will bring a cage with a living monkey inside, its head sticking out from above the cage held by the cage top at the neck so that the monkey cannot stir. Then the customer takes up a sharp knife and peel off the skin on the top of the monkey, and he takes up a small hammer to knock it on the monkey's head until its skulk breaks. Then he takes up a spoon to scoop a bit of the monkey's brain substance and dip it, still in the spoon, into the boiled water in the pot. He let it stay in the boiled water for a while and eat it. Genghua never witnessed such a brute action. They did not have much time to visit all the scenic spots in Canton. As in those days, Chinese people liked everything made abroad, Genghua bought a foreign-brand watch for his girlfriend. It was said the watch was smuggled in and so was affordable. When they got back to Shanghai, the relative returned to his own home and Genghua went to find the girl and gave her the watch.

When Genghua came back, Ahmei went home. During his absence, Ahmei had cleaned the two rooms, a small one and a big one. Genghua had slept in the small room before his father left. Now Ahmei had put his bed in the big room and re-arranged the furniture. The things that Genghua would not use were put away in the small room. Genghua used it as storeroom.

Now Genghua really lived alone. He stayed at home a lot, preparing teaching material for classes. Sometimes he bought food and ate at home. Since he was alone, he did not cook and just ate three meals anywhere he could get them. All his friends knew that he was alone, and so whenever he went to visit one, they would press Genghua to stay for supper.

Now Mr. Hu knew that Genghua would very probably go to Hong Kong, too, as he lived here alone. So he made a request to Genghua when one day they met in the campus. Mr. Hu wanted his son's *hukou* or household registration record entered into registration book of the house where Genghua was living, so that when Genghua went to Hong Kong, his son could move into his rooms. Otherwise, the housing department would take back the rooms and give then to some other family. Genghua could not refuse, and let his son put his name in his household registration book.

CHAPTER 21 – GENGHUA MARRIES

One day the girl asked Genghua to meet her father in a park. Mr. Cheng, her father, liked Genghua and told him that her daughter had a heart of gold, always treating people kindly. Being the youngest daughter, she had a little temper. That was okay with Genghua. He would not quarrel with a wife much younger than he. He doted on her.

Mr. Cheng had worked in the gas company owned by the British before the Party came to power. During the Japanese occupation of Shanghai, his British boss was put in a concentration camp. He had once gone there to visit him. Then he was arrested by the Japanese for supporting the strike of the workers. But the Japanese did not beat him. And after a few months, the Japanese surrendered and he came out. His British boss came out, too. So he went to work in the gas company again and his salary was raised. Before the Communist Party came into Shanghai, his British boss asked him to go with him to Hong Kong, but he did not comply. He had a big family to look after. His wife never worked and he had five younger sisters. When the Communist Party occupied Shanghai, they appointed him as the director of the supply department of the gas company, as he had helped to hide a Party member from being arrested by Chiang Kai-shek government, but his salary was greatly reduced, though still higher than most people there. He retired early as he had stomach and liver problems.

Mr. Cheng had five children. The eldest son graduated from Nanking Aeronautical Institute and was alloted a job in a factory in Shanghai. He was married and had two sons. His wife died of cancer. Mr. Cheng's second son studied in Tongji University for architecture, but when he graduated, he got kidney disease and one kidney was cut. So he lost the chance for the assignment of work and had to stay at home. Later he got a job as a shop assistant to sell soy sauce, salt, etc. He was married, too, and had a daughter. His wife worked in a so-called "lane productive group" and got the lowest pay. Mr. Cheng's third child was a daughter who graduated from Shanghai University of Finance & Economics and worked as the chief accountant in Shanghai Pharmaceutical Research Institute. Her husband was a teacher of Chinese history in a middle school. They also had a daughter. Mr. Cheng's fourth son graduated from Tangshan Railway Institute and went to work in Guiyang Town, Guizhou Province, in southwestern China. He was married to a girl in the same factory and had a daughter and a son. Mr. Cheng's youngest daughter Beili was Genghua's girlfriend and worked as a tracer of drafting in a lane productive group. Once she was "lent" to work in a factory, where she got to know Youfeng, the cousin of Genghua, their matchmaker.

In the Cultural Revolution, Mr. Cheng had also been put in jail. Some retired people, including Mr. Cheng, gathered in a park almost every day. They just sat there and chatted. But once they talked a little about Mao's wife and her former experience as an actress. Then one of them had some sort of trouble with the police and confessed about the talk. So all of them were arrested and sent to prison. Luckily, after half a year, the Gang of Four was apprehended and all those who were guilty of talking about Mao's wife were declared innocent and released.

From then on, Genghua was often invited to take supper in the house of his girlfriend. Her parents and neighbors pressed her to get married as soon as possible, because Genghua had two rooms. In those days in Shanghai, the most problem for marriage was whether the boy had housing, or at least the girl had housing. If the couple wanted to apply for a single room to the housing department, they must have certain conditions. If all their conditions met the requirements of the housing department, they would still have to wait, because there were so many couples in the same conditions. They had to get in a line on the list. It was an advantage for Genghua to have housing. So Genghua and Beili made all the preparations for wedding. They bought a set of new furniture and gave away the old ones to Ahmei, the former maidservant of the Wu family. As there was a long way from Genghua's home to the working place of Beili, they bought a small-size bike for her to ride to work. Then they went to the marriage department of the district government and got the marriage certificates on the twentieth of March, 1981. At last Genghua had a wife. Beili had rejected other men, younger than Genghua and with better conditions. One boy even came from Hong Kong. At that time girls in the mainland preferred to marry to those in Hong Kong or Macao, or better yet, abroad in other countries.

Then they went to a photo shop to take wedding pictures. The bride wore wedding costume. Genghua had a tuxedo made. A couple of days later, they invited relatives and friends to a restaurant for the wedding feast.

Guests coming from Beili's side were mostly her family members and relatives and her colleagues at work. Guests from Genghua's side were their matchmaker, her mother, her father being dead long ago in prison, her husband and daughter, then Mr. Hu and his family, and Ahmei with her family, as she had helped Genghua with the cleaning of the rooms and re-arrangement of the furniture. He did not invite any other friends, nor even his stepbrother. It was because when one day Genghua went to invite his stepbrother, who asked what he could give Genghua as wedding present, Genghua mentioned the TV set the stepbrother had promised their father to give it to Genghua. But the stepbrother said that he had already sold it to a friend of his. Genghua was unhappy about it. It was not the way it should be done. So Genghua did not invite the stepbrother.

After the wedding banquet, most guests dispersed to their respective homes. Only the colleagues of Beili, all boys, went with the newlywed to their home. A Chinese tradition allows guests attending a wedding ritual to play tricks on the newlywed on the wedding day. The tricks includes an apply hanging on a string from the ceiling and the couple should bite it from opposite side without using the hands. But there were no apples in Genghua's home. No tricks can be played without stage props. The colleagues could not find props for any of their purposes. But they found a square scarf and put it on the head of the bride. Then they asked Genghua, the bridegroom, to pick it up with a ruler like in the ancient days. Genghua wanted to stop their tricks at the very beginning. So he said with emphasis that he could not do that, afraid that he might blind the bride's eye by poking the ruler inside the scarf. He did not comply with their demand. So the tricks stopped here. They all sat down to have a chat till they left late in the night.

The next day, they woke up late and ate oranges, a real treat, for breakfast. Then they put candy into small bags. In the afternoon, they went to the house of her parents and stayed for supper, and returned home after it. They had three days' wedding leave. For those, either relatives or friends, who had not attended their wedding ritual, the couple would visit them with small bags of candy. It was another Chinese tradition. Genghua and his wife went to Genghua's friends one by one. They first reached Zhu family. Only a relative was there, the family all gone to Hong Kong. They went to see Dr. Jiang, whose niece Genghua had taught English had already left for the US. Next they visited Dong family, the daughter of which was like Queen Elisabeth. The mother said congratulations to the couple. Then they went to the Chen brothers to give them candy. Next day, Genghua took his wife to see Secretary Zhang, who had been assigned a leading position now. Then they went to Ni's house. The mother received them since Ni and his wife already went to Canada. They went to Wei's house. Doctor Wei already died of heart disease. His son complained that as a doctor he should not die like one without medical knowledge. When they went to Liu's house, they met the parents. His father was not a reactionary any more and began to work as a painter. The government wanted to sell his paintings to foreigners.

As they had to share the only full bathroom with two other families, it was inconvenient for Genghua and his wife. So they wanted to exchange housing, too. A couple of months later, they got a complicated exchange, four families involved. The first family moved to the place of the second family, who moved to the place of the third family, and the third family moved to where the fourth family lived while the fourth family moved to the housing of the first family. They had to move on the same day, or one of the families could not move into the place the family did not move on that day.

Now Genghua and his wife, Beili, lived in an apartment house on West Nanking Road, close to her workplace and her parents home. She could just walk wherever she needed to go, so she sold her bike. The location of their new home was in JingAn District. Now they had one room and two closets, one outside the room and one inside it. There was a bathroom attached, which for their use alone, inside their bedroom. What happiness!

One Sunday they went to Guyi Garden for sightseeing. The garden was situated in the small town, Nanxiang (meaning "Flying South"), about 20 kilometers away, northwest of Shanghai. It was also famous for its juicy mantou (steamed bun with a minced meat). The beautiful ancient garden—Guqi Garden—was originally build in Ming Dynasty, between 1522–1566 AD, during the reign of Emperor Jiajing, bearing the name of Yi Garden. But in Qing Dynasty, in 1746, the eleventh year of the reign of Emperor Qianlong, it was repaired and then renamed Guyi Garden.

The garden is so arranged, with the Playing Goose Pond as its center, the White Stork Arbor to the west, the Stone Boat to the north and the Floating Bamboo Pavilion to the south. According to a legend in Liang Dynasty, between 502—577 AD, a big white stone, about three meters long, was accidentally unearthed and then two white storks were often seen flying down to have a respite on top of the stone. Many years later, a monk by the name of Deqi came by and saw them, thinking that it was a good place to build a temple on since white storks rested on the white stone. Therefore, a temple was built in the neighborhood, and soon afterwards, the white storks flew south and never came back again. So the temple was named "White-Stork-Flying-South" Temple in memory of the two storks. Later around the temple a small town grew. Hence, it bore the name of the "Flying-South" Town. In Ming Dynasty, an arbor was set up where the storks were said once rested, which was then given the name of "White Stork Arbor".

The couple sat in the arbor for a while, then stepped onto a small footpath leading northeast to the Stone Boat, also built in Ming Dynasty. In the cabin hangs a wooden plateau high up on the wall opposite to the door, on which are inscribed three Chinese characters: "Non-Tied Boat." Genghua knew that these characters were taken from an article by Chuancius (369—286 BC), an ancient essayist and philosopher in Zhou Dynasty. He explained to Beili. It was said that this plateau was put up after 1949, the original one being lost during the Anti-Japanese War and to the disappointment of visitors, because the original three Chinese characters were written by the prominent calligrapher Zhu Zhishan (1460—1526 AD) of Ming Dynasty. Above the cabin is a small pavilion used as a study by the original owner. But the staircase was blocked and no visitors could go upstairs.

There across another pond, to the west of the White Stork Arbor, stands a pavilion known as Hermitage Pavilion, with windows all around and some beautifully carved furniture in it, and also with two trees in front and two at one side—a rare variety of ash-tree (Var Pendula Loud)—which was said could only be grown in the palace of the emperor. If any was found planted in the garden of anyone, no matter whether courtiers of the highest rank or people of the lowest class, he would be put to death on the accusation that he had the intention to become the emperor himself—the greatest crime of treason and revolt. So the original owner of the garden was beheaded on account of the trees. But Genghua thought of those innocent people killed nowadays.

A little south from Hermitage Pavilion is another pavilion called "Flying-Kite-and-Jumping-Fish" Pavilion, built also in Ming Dynasty. Originally it was a straw-thatched hut facing a small pool and sitting in it one could see kites flying above and fish jumping below; hence, the name. But the present pavilion was rebuilt in 1974.

South to Floating Bamboo Pavilion, up on the small "Bamboo-Branch" Mound, stands another arbor, "One-Corner-Lacking" Arbor, built in 1931, after the 9.18 (September 18th) Event, with the lacking corner of the roof pointing to the northeast to remind people of the event and the other three corners raised up like high-raised arms and clenched fists to symbolize the people's will of resistance against Japanese invasion. Genghua took a photo of it with his wife standing in front.

Further south, over a little bigger pond spans a zigzagged bridge with an arbor on it in the middle that visitors can sit in it and get a view of the beautiful surroundings. Genghua took another photo of Beili sitting in the arbor. East to One-Corner-Lacking Arbor, another pavilion can be seen with the name of "Plum-Blossom" Pavilion, built in Qing Dynasty, but now serves as a shop selling works of arts. Articles sold at scenic spots always cost more than their true values. Genghua and his wife did not buy anything. Before and behind it, some plum trees burst into bloom with the season, and in the south of the garden one can still see the peony grown there a little before the reign of Empress Dowager of Qing Dynasty, perhaps, when she was only an imperial concubine.

There are two octagonal stone columns about three meters tall, shaped somewhat like pagodas, one in the northeastern part of the garden and the other to the west of One-corner-Lacking Arbor. The work of building them began in 867 AD and ended in 875 AD in Tang Dynasty, eight years it took, and known as Sutra Column of Tang Dynasty. They were repaired in 980 AD in Song Dynasty. The one in the northeastern part has only four Buddhas inscribed on it, but on the other, besides four Buddhas, there are characters of Sutra carved on it, which was re-inscribed in Yuan Dynasty, in 1333 AD. However, in 1790 AD, the fifty-fourth year of the reign of Emperor Qianlong of Qing Dynasty, it was brought down by typhoon and in 1800, the fifth year of reign of Emperor Jiaqing, son of Emperor Qianlong, it was re-set up with four Buddhas and the Sutra characters inscribed on it again. Both columns were removed here in 1959 from the ruins of the Hovering-Cloud Temple.

East of Plum-blossom Pavilion, standing in the water of the Lotus Pond is a column-like pagoda, about two meters high above the water surface, built in 1222 AD in Song Dynasty, which is called Common Pagoda. There are two kinds of pagodas: one has many storeys and people can go in and climb up one storey after another to have a long view from its windows, and the other is just a stone pillar to hold inside it an urn containing a monk's ashes or with Buddhas or Sutra characters engraved on its sides. Common Pagoda belongs to the latter sort.

In the garden there are a few artificial grottoes, and also other pavilions, such as South Pavilion, Stork-Longevity Pavilion, Moon-Portraying Pavilion, and Faint-Sound Pavilion, which is now a shop selling sweets, drinks and ice-cream, etc. Before 1949, the garden with all its buildings was seriously damaged and so after 1949 it was repaired several times. Just inside the front gate a brick wall about five meters wide and two meters high shuts out the view of the garden and visitors had to get round it to have a full sight. The wall has a relief on it. There are also a tea room and a canteen in which visitors can enjoy the famous delicious mantou. In the eastern corner, two white storks are resting there, supposedly returning from the south after so many years of absence. Storks are said to be the symbol of longevity. May those who take photos with the two storks there enjoy health and longevity!

Mr. Hu wanted a promotion to be an associate professor. He was then only a lecturer. But there was one condition for the promotion that the person should have mastered thoroughly a foreign language, like English or German or Japanese. The proof of it should be some translated articles in that foreign language to be published in some magazines. Mr. Hu had majored in geography and his English was poor and he could not translate anything. So he asked Genghua to translate some geography articles in an English magazine into Chinese so that he could get them published. Genghua did as he was bid.

As Genghua was still a temporary teacher without any health benefits, his wife thought that it would be better for them to apply to go to Hong Kong. So they sent in application forms to their police branch. The policeman in charge of their block was Comrade Chen. He was a national model policeman and very kind to Genghua and his wife, since he knew that Genghua had contact in the municipal police station.

Beili and her colleagues came and left freely in their working place. So she went to the reception room in JingAn police precinct from time to time to learn if their applications were approved. A man receptionist hinted about his desire for money. But Genghua and Beili did not like the idea. After a few months when Beili went there again, there was a new receptionist. A rumor went that the former receptionist had killed himself for taking bribes.

A few months later, Beili found herself with child. Now Genghua needed more money. He began to teach private pupils at home. All his pupils came to learn TOEFL testing skills. They all had the intention to go to the US. Most of these pupils came from special families. Only children from special families could afford to go to the US. One girl's father was a famous surgeon in the Sixth People's Hospital, who could re-connect broken arms or fingers. Her mother was the superintendent of the Ninth People's Hospital. Before long, the girl went to the US and later became a plastic surgeon with an office in New York.

Shanghai Foreign Languages Institute established an affiliate unit called Shanghai Foreign Languages Educational Press. Mr. Hu knew the director of the Press and recommended Genghua to work there as a part-time editor, literally called "Specially Invited Editor," to earn some more money. Of course, at every major festival, Genghua would take some gifts to see the director. Genghua worked with a full-time editor, a Mr. Li, who suggested to compile a book as reading material for university students, titled Literary Gems For Recitation. They selected many famous essays, poems and short stories in English. They planned to translate all the stuff into Chinese and put both language versions side by side in publication. As a joke, Genghua mingled his own compositions in the materials, a poem titled *To Spring* and an essay *On Etiquette*. He wanted to see if anyone could distinguish them from the works of ancient people. But to their disappointment, the chief editor changed his mind and wanted them to transfer the materials to a professor in Shanghai Normal University. Genghua waited to see whether this so-called professor could tell his poem and essay from others by ancient foreign writers and poets. Of course, he could not use his own name for them. He used Hazlitt for his essay and Longfellow for his poem. When the book was published, Genghua found that both his essay and poem were there.

The poem *To Spring* concluded as follows:

> May seasons all be Spring—the pride of years,
> That all things would e'er in glories gleam!
> May men be ever in the prime of years!
> But a dream, however sweet, is but a dream.
> If you're happy when you come and sad when gone,
> Would that you'd never come—or never gone!

As a professor of Chinese literature, the compiler should have known that the last two lines expressed a typical Chinese idea. So should the editor. But neither one sensed that something was out of place, and they published it accordingly.

Since Beili's work group ignored the work rules, their immediate leaders wanted to dismiss the group and sent individuals to work in some other groups. One leader remembered that once he went there for inspection, they gave him a piece of candy. But when he unwrapped it and put the candy into his mouth, the taste was like soap. It was a piece of soap cut like candy and wrapped in candy paper. They often played practical jokes on leaders they detested.

Now all the group members took sick leave. So did Beili, who was sent to work in a group requiring hard labor. When Beili went to talk to the leader that they had to give her light work as she was now pregnant, they rejected her request. So Genghua went to see Secretary Zhang he had known before and asked her to hand in a letter of petition. Secretary Zhang promised to turn in the letter to a vice director of Shanghai Women's Federation. Then, when the girl pupil came to have the lesson, Beili told her about her situation, the girl said that her mother knew a leader in the district government and could hand in a letter for that matter. So Genghua wrote a letter of the same contents. The girl took the letter to her mother, who gave it to the leader she knew.

Meanwhile a girl worker in Beili's group suddenly committed suicide. She was an introversive girl and could not bear any pressure. When all this was added up, the leaders had to take back their decision and let the group work as before. But later the group was changed from drafting to a packing job. They would pack products into bales for other factories as those factory masters did not want to set up a packing group of their own. Beili worked as a liaison. She should find packing work for the group. She had two sources to fulfill her task: one from the factory she had worked for and the other from the factory her eldest brother was the vice factory master. As long as she fulfilled her task, Beili could stay at home for the rest of the week.

CHAPTER 23 – DREAMS COME TRUE

One day Genghua got a letter from Bai saying that he would soon come to Shanghai and stay in Jinjiang Hotel on the corner of Ruijin Road and Changle Road. When Genghua moved to the new location, he had written to Bai with the change of address. Bai also said in his letter that he would come to visit Genghua on the day after he arrived in Shanghai. So Genghua and his wife were prepared to treat their guest with crabs and other special dishes.

On the appointed date, Bai did make his appearance. It was the first time Bai had come to Shanghai in all these years. Genghua introduced his wife to him and Bai showed photos of his wife, who had stayed in Germany with their son. Each told the other how they had fared during their separation. Then they talked about raising children. Bai gave an example that someone having not been brought up properly would behave like this: when he bought a new expensive car, he would bang his car door heavily to attract public attention to his new car to show that he was a rich man while a well-educated person would not do that. The next evening Bai invited them for dinner in a restaurant in Jinjiang Hotel. In those days, not everyone could go into that kind of restaurant, which was only open to foreigners. Bai came out to walk them in as invited guests. The prices of the dishes were much higher than those in ordinary restaurants. In countries with non-convertible currency, everything has two sets of standards, one for foreigners and one for local people. Genghua and his wife enjoyed the dinner very much.

Bai had come to Shanghai this time with a certain goal. The company he worked with planned to open a branch office in Shanghai and wanted Bai to look for a person to be the manager here. Naturally Bai had thought of Genghua. But the government policy was that Bai had to hire such a person through a government office, which would send Bai a person they chose. Bai had no right to employ anyone he liked. So Genghua could not go for it.

After a few years of teaching the test skills, Genghua wrote a book with the title of *TOEFL Testing Skills*. By chance, a former neighbor of Beili was married to a leader in the publishing bureau. He sent Genghua to see an editor working with Shanghai Translation Publishing House. The publishing house decided to publish it immediately since there were so many people taking TOEFL at that time. Genghua and the editor worked on the book, which came out faster than expected and sold well. The first editions sold 50,000 copies and the second edition 30,000 copies. But the royalty he got was only 900 yuan of Chinese currency. At that time, a publisher only gave the author a lump sum of money, no royalties.

Then the Shanghai Second Medical College and East China Textile College invited Genghua to teach his testing skills in their colleges, so he earned some more money.

There was a private college called Shanghai Advanced College of Continuing Education. In China, universities and colleges belonged to the government. But after the open policy was carried out, private colleges were permitted. The college gave classes about TOEFL as it was so popular, particularly in Shanghai. A fellow lady teacher in Genghua's office recommended Genghua to Mr. Cai, the organizer of that college. When Mr. Cai was told that Genghua was teaching TOEFL testing skills, he was greatly interested and asked Genghua to teach the skills to his students. The time of the class was every Sunday morning, from eight to twelve at noon, in the auditorium of the Children's Hall of Changning District. It had 500 seats. It seemed that Genghua was giving a lecture to round 400 students. Like always, he let the students do the test first and then explain to them how to use the skills in TOEFL tests. Students welcomed his test skills teaching. So Mr. Cai increased his pay. Now Genghua had more than one job at the time. Only they all were temporary.

Genghua got another pupil recommended to him by the sister of Beili. The young man's brother was a colleague of Beili's sister, and was also the son-in-law of Cao Diqiu, the former mayor of Shanghai, who died in the Cultural Revolution. At first the young man wanted to go to the US and so learn TOEFL testing skills. But after a while he changed his mind and went to Japan. At that time, a cousin of Beili was in Japan. So Beili told the young man how to get in touch with her cousin so that the new arrival could have someone to help him if he needed it.

Another pupil came to Genghua's home to learn English from him. Later Genghua learned that his uncle was a vice minister of Shanghai United Front Work Department. So Genghua requested him for the help with either of the problems before him: either to approve their applications to Hong Kong, or to get a permanent job in the university. The pupil said that if Genghua needed the help from United Front Work Department, his father's name should be in their list, i.e., he should be a person with certain political status. So Genghua went to check on the old newspapers in the library of the university and did find his father's name on it as the people's representative of the conference in Shanghai. So he wrote a letter for the pupil to give to his uncle. But several months passed without any result.

A professor, by the surname of Huang, came to see Genghua. He would soon take APT test given by the Education Ministry for sending students or professors to the US as visiting scholars. TOEFL testing skills could be used in APT test as well. Prof. Huang knew the director of the Night School of East China Normal University. The director recommended him to Genghua. So Genghua taught all the skills to him and he did pass the test and was sent as a visiting scholar to Rutgers University in New Jersey. His wife Dr. Sophie Jiang came to thank Genghua and his wife. She became a good friend of Beili.

When the time drew near for Beili to give birth Dr. Jiang recommended her to the Renji Hospital where she worked as a pediatrician. She would ask a colleague of hers, a gynecologist, to take special care of Beili. As she was a woman of Advanced Reproductive Age and her husband was over forty, their child must be guaranteed for a safe birth.

And so a girl was born, another dream come true. Genghua did not care if it was a girl or a boy. While it may be true that a boy child carries on the family name, Genghua understood that the one-child policy might have been correct for China at that time. Mao had encouraged people to have more children, as the Soviet Union had done after massive losses in the two World Wars, but in China population growth was disastrous, accentuating the pressures of overpopulation and difficulties with food supply. After the first and the Second World War, the population of the Soviet Union had been decimated twice over, and they needed to recover. Not China. (As of today, China has already been able to begin easing back on the one-child policy, having rectified one more of Mao's excessive measures.)

Beili stayed in the hospital for a few days and Genghua took her home in a taxi. The girl was born on the eighteenth day of the sixth moon of lunar calendar, in 1982, the year of dog. She slept in a crib. Some parents will keep the baby in bed between them, but accidents have happened.

According to Chinese tradition, Beili had to lie in bed for a month. During the first few days, her mother came to look after her. Then a woman her family knew offered to come to take care of her. She worked as a dry nurse. Genghua paid her for her help. According to Chinese custom, a baby had a formal name used in official record and a nickname or a pet name used at home. There was an English teaching program on television just at that time. The female character was called Linda. So Genghua used Linda as the baby's pet name.

In fact, by then Genghua was thinking of himself as "Frank," and projecting himself more and more into the English-speaking world. All his work in studying English was finally about to open the door to his dream.

China wanted to send more students and visiting scholars to the US to learn advanced science and technology. Therefore, the Education Ministry of the State Council determined to establish two centers: TOEFL research center and GRE research center. The TOEFL research center was in Canton and the GRE research center was in Shanghai, in East China Normal University. Mr. Hu knew some leader in the education ministry and he guaranteed the full support of the university to the research work. So the education ministry agreed to set up the GRE center here. Now Frank belonged to the GRE center, though he still taught TOEFL.

The education ministry planned to have a meeting in XiAn Foreign Languages Institute in XiAn City. Mr. Chi, the director, and Frank were assigned to attend the meeting. Before the formal meeting began in XiAn City, there was a preliminary meeting held in the East China Normal University, Shanghai. So Frank got acquainted with all the attenders. After that, the formal meeting would soon begin in XiAn City. Mr. Chi and Frank took a train there. At the meeting they discussed the research work on TOEFL and GRE tests. At the interval between meetings the institute authorities took all the meeting attenders to have a tour in their institute bus.

XiAn is an old city, and also a city with many relics because it was one of the capitals of many dynasties in ancient China. Therefore, in and around the city, there are many relics such as Drum Pavilion, Bell Pavilion, Big Wild Goose Pagoda, Small Wild Goose Pagoda, the Museum of Stone Tablets, the Tomb of the First Emperor of Qin Dynasty, the Vaults of Terra-cotta Warriors and Horses, the Tomb of Empress Wu the Great of the Tang Dynasty, the Tomb of Princess Yongtai of Tang Dynasty and Huaqing Pool, etc.

The first place they went was the Vaults of Terra-cotta Warriors and Horses, situated some 1.5 km east of the Tomb of the First Emperor of Qin Dynasty, three vaults on display and many others being dug. All warriors, as well as horses, are lifelike and lifesize, some holding bronze spears and some carrying bows and arrows, and others following chariots, all in war array. According to the estimation of experts, there are 8,000 figures and horses, and over 100 chariots. These warriors were buried there as bodyguards to the Emperor. People in the old time of China believed that when one died his ghost would live in the nether world just as he had lived in the upper world. So his sons would put into the tomb all the clothes, jewelry and utensils he needed in his life in the darkness. If he was an emperor, his sons would in addition have clay warriors and horses made and buried near his tomb to protect him from any danger of being attacked by other sovereign ghosts. The heads of the figures are movable and removable. Figures wearing caps of different shapes are officers of different ranks while those without caps are soldiers. It can be said without boasting that it is the eighth wonder of the world, considering the number, the size and the workmanship.

Huaqing Pool, located at the foot of Lishan Mountain, is famous for the pool, in which Yang Yuhuan (died in 755 AD), the imperial concubine of Emperor Xuanzong of Tang Dynasty (on the throne: 712–755 AD), often came to take her bath. The pool is in a small room, made of smooth stone and shaped like a four-petaled flower. But the additional buildings there are not constructed in Tang Dynasty. The original ones were destroyed during the wars waged by subsequent dynasties and the present ones were rebuilt later. It was said that before the imperial concubine came from the palace, the guardsmen held up two lines on either side from which cloth hung down to form a passageway so that no one, maybe by chance in the vicinity, could see her.

The whole place of Huaqing Pool is a beautiful garden with flowers and trees, a pond and pavilions in it. There are also rows of small bathrooms where a visitor can take a hot spring water bath by paying for a ticket. It is good for one's health. The temperature of the water is just a little higher than that of normal human body. But most visitors have no time for that—they have to hurry to the next site on the tourist plan.

Near the pool, in the same bungalow, is the room in which Chiang Kai-shek stayed during the XiAn Incident in 1936. Nearly halfway up the hillside stands a stone arbor called "Catch-Chiang" Arbor. During the night the incident happened, when Chiang Kai-shek heard the report of guns, he quickly climbed out of the back window and ran barefoot as fast as he could up the hill. He hid himself in a crevice of the rock near the arbor, where he was found and taken prisoner; hence the name of the arbor.

On Lishan Mountain there used to be a beacon tower in West Zhou Dynasty. A story goes back to that time about the tower. The queen of King You, the last king of West Zhou Dynasty (on the throne: 781–771 BC), never even smiled in her life. The king tried every means in his power to make her smile, but his efforts were all in vain. He asked her what she had liked best as a little girl. She said that she liked to hear the sound of tearing cloth. So the king ordered many scrolls of expensive cloth to be brought into the palace and had them torn one by one into shreds, but the queen still didn't smile. Once he took her there on the mountain. When they stood on the top, a wonderful idea struck him. He ordered his men to ignite the beacon fire, a signal to summon the lords for help when foreign aggression happened. Accordingly, the lords hurried there with their troops, banners upheld and drums sounding, thinking that the enemies invaded the kingdom again. When they saw only the king and queen sitting on the summit, they looked at one another and hurried away with banners rolled up and drums muffled. At last the queen smiled—such a sweet smile that made her look even more beautiful and attractive. But later, when enemies actually invaded and the beacon fire was lit, no one came to the rescue, and the king was killed and the queen was captured. So the tale of the one who cried wolf is present in Chinese legends as well.

The Tomb of Empress Wu the Great, situated west of XiAn City, has not been explored yet. Empress Wu in Tang Dynasty was the first and the last female sovereign, that is to say, the sole female sovereign in the long history of China. In the Chinese feudal society, the status of women was so low that they were dependent on their parents as a girl, on their husbands after marriage and on their sons as a widow. It was against the convention and conception of feudal-ism that a woman could be a sovereign, but Empress Wu managed to be one and maintained her reign for so many years. There must have been something that we can learn. According to history, she chose upright men to be her courtiers and made wise policies in the interests of people. These might account for her long reign. By her order, given before her death, a tall stone tablet was put up posthu-mously at one side in front of her tomb without any Chinese char-acters engraved on it. She would leave it for the posterity to inscribe whatever comments they would make on her merits or demerits. This tablet is called "No Word Tablet."

Not far from her tomb is the tome of Princess Yongtai, her granddaughter, now open to visitors. Through a declining passage-way, they went down into the innermost part of the tomb, where the princess's coffin stands. On the walls of the passageway some pretty frescoes were seen. Two exhibition halls were set up on each side of the tomb in the foreground, in which on display are all the things taken from the tomb; among them are the well-known three-colored porcelain camels, horses and figurines of Tang Dynasty. One camel of a larger size carries some smaller figurines on its back, its head raised high and the figurines all playing musical instruments except one woman in the middle. She was singing. An interpreter was explaining to some foreign visitors, and in the end he added, "The woman in the middle is singing and the camel is singing, too." And laughter rose among the listeners.

The museum of XiAn is in the city. Besides the famous three-colored porcelain figurines, the exhibition includes a few coins of ancient Persia and some earthenware of thousands of years ago found underground, etc. But the chief exhibition is the sculptures and engravings in stone: squatting stone lions and other stone ani-mals bigger than lifesize, stone coffins, stone Buddhas, stone drag-ons and deer in relief and mostly stone tablets of different dynasties and different sizes, a few tablets with stone turtles under them, of course, in one piece. Whole books and articles were inscribed on them. Therefore, these have often been imitated since then by the learners of calligraphy. Chinese calligraphy is also a fine art and always goes hand in hand with Chinese paintings while the tablet is a thesaurus for Chinese calligraphy to be kept and handed down.

The meeting ended after a week and the attendees from other cities went back to where they had come from. Mr. Chi and Frank came back to Shanghai. Frank had bought some small toys for his daughter.

Mr. Chi was applying to go to the US as a visiting scholar. He wished to take something there to show his talent. As he knew that Frank had a good command of English, he asked Frank to translate the famous book "Art of War" by Suntze, a strategist in military affairs in the Wu Kingdom in the sixth century BC. So Frank translated the book from Chinese into English for him, and Mr. Chi took the translation to the US.

Mr. Hu's wife invited Frank and his wife to dine in their home. Mr. Hu had a son and two daughters. All of them had work, but not married yet. Beili liked fun to mix with other people. She loved to eat at the home of other people without cooking by herself. It was a Chinese custom that when people invited anyone to dinner at home, the one invited should buy something, such as a bag of fruit or candy, or even a bottle of wine, to take to the family. So did Frank and his wife. During the , Mrs. Hu asked Beili about their future and Beili told her that it seemed impossible they would ever get their permission to travel to Hong Kong. When Mr. Hu heard this, he was unhappy. If they could not go to Hong Kong, especially when they had a child, Mr. Hu's son would never get Frank's room. Mr. Hu's good plans would go up in smoke. So a year later, Mr. Hu took back his son's hukou or residence record and entered it into their own household registration book. Relations were no longer close between the two families.

One day Mr. Hu brought a man to Frank's home. After the introductions, Genghua understood that this was the Mr. Jiang who worked in Shanghai Normal University, who was the brother of the Municipal Party Secretary Jiang Zeming, later the secretary general of the Central Party Committee. Why did Mr. Hu bring the man to Frank's home? Because his own home looked too shabby. They were discussing the need to establish a second TOEFL and GRE test center in Shanghai, preferably in the west of the city, as the first center was already functioning at the Shanghai Foreign Languages Institute in the east part of Shanghai. Mr. Hu wanted it to be set up either in Shanghai Normal University or in East China Normal University. He apparently wanted this Mr. Jiang to use his brother's influence. Anyway, the test center was established in the latter. And even so, Mr. Hu did not secure one of the permanent positions for Frank, though he was so deeply involved in the project.

Comrade Luo and Comrade Jin had gone to the High Education Bureau to negotiate with the cadres there for a permanent position to be given to Frank, but no success. Chinese officials always insist in their decision, even if it is wrong. Frank looked upon it as fated. As things developed, it was his fate that he was a temporary. If he was a permanent, the authorities in his university would never let him go since he taught such important lessons. It was because when he was a permanent, he had to be approved by the university authorities to apply for a passport. Now as he was only a temporary, he could apply without approval needed from the university he was working for.

Linda was three years old now. She went to kindergarten. Her mother took her there in the morning and picked her in the evening. She began to learn reading and writing Chinese characters. Most times, children there just played. Teachers in kindergartens are always females. One teacher does all the teaching work in the curriculum. Once the teacher of the class Linda was in took all the children to a gymnasium to sing in a chorus. Frank and Beili went there to watch. There was no stage and the children just stood in the center of the arena, singing the song they had been taught in the class.

One day, Dr. Sophie Jiang came to bid farewell to Frank and Beili. She would go to the US on J-2 visa with her two daughters. She offered to help Beili and Frank get invitation letters, certain forms and documents as well.

Almost half a year later, Frank got all the documents he needed to apply for a passport, and he sent in his application to go to the United States. He contacted Comrade Luo and Comrade Jin and told them all about it. Since they could not help him to solve the problem of becoming a permanent teacher, they supported him to go to the United States. So they went to the police station and got a passport for Frank in a few days. Then he went to the US consulate in Shanghai and got a J-1 visa as a visiting scholar to Rutgers University in New Jersey. The tide had finally turned in Frank's favor.

A former pupil from Nanking came back for a visit and, when he learned that Frank would soon be leaving, he invited the whole family for a tour of Nanking. So Frank and his wife and daughter took the train back to Nanking with the pupil and stayed in the home of this pupil, who lived with his sister's family. His brother-in-law was a driver of a van and so they drove Frank's family all around the sites of Nanking City.

The first place they visited was the Mausoleum of Dr. Sun Yat-sen, located at the foot of Rose Gold Mountain. A famous revolutionary, Sun Yat-sen worked to overthrow China's last imperial dynasty and in 1912 proclaimed the Republic of China. This was a period of civil war, invasions by Japan and other disturbances. By 1920 Dr. Sun had reformulated his party as the Kuomintang. After a series of successes and setbacks, alliances and betrayals, with varying support from Chinese warlords and the Soviet Union, he laid the foundations of a competing view of what the nation of China should be; he died of cancer in Beijing in 1925. His successor Chiang Kai-shek eventually fled with his supporters to the island of Formosa, and created there what is now known as Taiwan. Recent research has revealed that Dr. Sun Yat-sen was in fact an American citizen, suggesting that our understanding of these episodes of history is incomplete.

Next stop was the Rain-Flower Terrace situated in the south suburb of Nanking. The legend handed down was like this: During the rule of King Wu of Liang Kingdom in the Southern Dynasties, Monk YunGuang set up a terrace here to give speeches on Buddhist sutras. He spoke so touchingly that Heaven was moved and let flowers rain down. Hence, the name. There is a museum with Rain-Flower Stones on display. Those multi-colored stones, polished by the waters of the Yangtze, are sometimes called picture pebbles. Every one has a different pattern, looking like moss hanging from trees in the mist, or a slice of salmon sushi, or a scattering of brilliant bulls' eyes, all naturally-formed variations of quartz. A showcase holds the best Rain-Flower stones that a private collector has lent to the museum for display.

They stayed only for three days in Nanking. Frank had to hurry back for classes. Once back, they made all the preparations for the long journey to the US. Beili bought all the things necessary for the travel, heavy coat and such stuffs. Frank was only allowed to exchange forty dollars from the People's Bank. That year, Frank was fifty and Linda was five. Beili's family all gathered in a restaurant to celebrate Frank's fiftieth birthday and congratulated him for being able to go to the US, a new start in life. At the end of November, 1987, he took an airplane to the US, fulfilling the dream he'd cherished for decades. Half a year later, Beili and Linda followed. The family united in America, with visions of flowers, even in the rain.